My Wife is Married to a Feckin' Eejit

Bernard O'Shea

Gill Books

Gill Books
Hume Avenue
Park West
Dublin 12
www.gillbooks.ie

Gill Books is an imprint of M.H. Gill and Co.

978 07171 8387 6

Design and print origination by O'K Graphic Design, Dublin
Copy-edited by Jane Rogers
Proofread by Esther Ní Dhonnacha
Printed in the U.K. by Clays Ltd, Elcograf S.p.A

This book is typeset in 13.5/17 pt Minion.

The paper used in this book comes from the wood pulp of managed forests. For
every tree felled, at least one tree is planted, thereby renewing natural resources.

A CIP catalogue record for this book is available from the British Library.

5 4 3 2

About the Author

Bernard O'Shea is an Irish comedian and broadcaster from Durrow, County Laois. In radio he wrote sketches for Today FM and co-hosted two breakfast shows on iRadio and 2FM. In television he first made his name on RTÉ's *The Republic of Telly*, co-wrote and co-starred in the sitcom *Bridget & Eamon*, and more recently can be seen in *Marty and Bernard's Big Adventure*. In the course of his stand-up career he won the Harp Newcomer Comedy Award in 2000 and performed in the BBC Newcomer Awards the same year. He has performed at comedy festivals around the world, including Montreal and Edinburgh. He currently lives in Dublin with his long-suffering wife and three children, and is a full-time comedy writer and performer.

Thank you to my family, friends and colleagues,
especially my wife, Lorna, and kids,
Olivia, Tadhg and Seán

Introduction

Sunday 9 September 2007 was one of the luckiest days of my life. I didn't actually know this, because I had to ask my wife, Lorna, 'When did I first meet you?' Her answer was: Sunday 9 September 2007. My question sums up this book. Just eight months previously, on 1 January, I had been extracted from a large shrub outside a petrol station in Ranelagh, Dublin, where I was living at the time. I was covered in corn flakes and drenched in milk. After a particularly heavy New Year's Eve celebration, I had bought cereal and milk from the 24-hour shop in the petrol station and decided that an overgrown conifer made a perfect place to spend the night, even though I lived just across the road.

It might seem like shabby accommodation, but it was a step up from the bedsit that I had lived in for the previous three years. I had no job, no money and most certainly no girlfriend. I was the most single man in Ireland. I was also trying to become a stand-up comedian and was failing miserably. My gigs were up and down, mostly down. I was the man who had nothing going for him. Red hair, pale skin and a beer belly. I was living the dream.

On New Year's Day 2007, I made two decisions: to give up 'the drink' and give comedy one last heave-ho. I have decided that every New Year's Day since. The only difference is that I have an accomplice now. My wife. We also have three children.

For me, life is a lazy adventure, but for my wife it's more of an endurance race. I'm not a great husband; my parenting skills lack, well, skill. Yet somehow, the yin and yang of our relationship works – for me, anyway. My wife is a planner, a bill payer, a child washer, a future-proofer, and I am not. What I bring to the table is fun or anxiety, depending on the day and the mood I'm in. She has joked that she has running-away money. I've started contributing to it as she will have to bring me with her, because I wouldn't survive on my own with the kids. Through nearly twelve years of fights and flights, holiday disasters and toddler tantrums, we have just about survived.

Relationships aren't easy and I know this because I asked my wife to tell me the top three most stupid things I've ever done. Within seconds, she listed twenty. I should have been offended, but I thought – only twenty? Later, when I was in her good room, the one that's out of bounds to the kids, sitting on her nice clean sofa while she was out at work, I found her diary. It was wedged under a cushion. They always say you should never read anyone else's diary, which is practically demanding that you do, so I did. 'Bernard asked me to list all the stupid, idiotic things he's ever done,' the first sentence read, and beneath it was a list. 'Stupid idiotic things Bernard has done.' When I confronted her, her justification was 'I am married to a f##king eejit … I need to take notes.' This book is the list she had written, and I've added a few that she didn't think of.

PART ONE

A Trial Run for Eejitry

1. He told me that he once shaved his pubic hair.

I used to think that I had edited my past so that Lorna only knew the good stuff. I wanted her to think that I was a grown-up when she met me (in spite of the New Year's Day conifer incident), a fully fledged human with whom she could be seen in daylight and not be mortified. I was wrong. I have no idea how she found out about the shaving of more than my face, but she did, as I can see from the diary that she thinks I don't know about. And it was the number one thing on her list of things that annoyed her about me. Let me explain.

I was never obsessed with my looks or clothes until I got older and noticed that my clothes didn't fit me any more, due to my expanding waistline, and that my red hair, which was once overly abundant, was disappearing due to a receding hairline and reappearing out of my nose and ears. My mum has always been stylish and had a clothes shop when I was growing up. My three older sisters always liked clothes and I think were partially responsible for Ireland's economic downturn in '08 due to their phenomenal spending sprees. My dad was also obsessive about his clothes. I, however, didn't catch the clothes bug at all. I've always bought clothes that were functional. Essentially, I would love to wear work pants and army jackets with lot of pockets, but after a brief spell in the early nineties, this is not fashionable any more. It's hard to be a fashionista anyway when you have my looks. Now some people, hopefully my wife, love how I look, or looked, but I'm very, very, very, very, very Irish looking. I've extremely pale skin that burns when people just talk about good weather. I've green-brown eyes and red hair. My hair isn't curly or full of waves; it's ditch hair. By ditch hair, I mean that it's just thick and grows – or at least grew – thick; not down, just out. It used to grow at such a rate that I would have to go to a different barber every two weeks, because I got so fed up with having the same conversation with the barber: 'Were you here last week?' I'd reply 'Yeah', and as usual the response would be something like 'Jaysus, what are ya eating? I scalped you the last time.' Thus, I had burned into my brain a *Lord of the Rings*-style mental map of Dublin barbers that I would frequent in rotation every fortnight to avoid the conversation.

On the hairy subject, the one thing I hate about being a man is shaving. I remember my first shave. I used a razor so old that I was lucky not to have got sepsis. I remember thinking, 'Do I have to do this every day?' 'Yes' was the answer. I have basically no chest hair or body hair, but Christ almighty, from the age of thirteen, I would shave in the morning and have stubble by noon. It's a pain in the arse. By the time I left college and embarked on a career of bedsit-living and comedy training I always had some kind of beard, mostly down to outright laziness. Those ads for razors don't show the reality. No matter how many blades you have on your razor your partner will never seductively give you a reach around and feel how smooth your skin is. Even now, my hair repels most products. When it comes into contact with gel or hair wax, it just absorbs them, and I can't style it. It's like my hair is telling me, 'Listen here, buddy, you're a culchie. Don't be getting any ideas.'

But there is one universal truth to every man's follicular life journey. He decides at some point to take a little bit off down below. It has become something of the norm for women to have trimmed pubic hair, but men have been slow to this pubic containment procedure. If I'm being honest, most men will think, 'Maybe it will look bigger if I trim around it.' Well, that's what I thought, but it took me years to finally decide to clean up my mangrove.

One Sunday morning, I decided I would give it a go. I got into the shower and started clipping away. The absolute fear of going near that region with a scissors and a razor blade filled me with dread, but I was at a mental point where I had to do it. I was compelled to. It almost felt as if I would be imbued with superhero power if I did, almost like a reversal of the story of Samson in the Bible. But like a tube of Pringles, once I started, I just couldn't stop. I kept telling myself, 'Stop, it looks weird now,' but I couldn't. I was trying to even it up on both sides, but I ended up basically testicularly bald, with some hair left on my right side. In my desperation I started to do a comb-over. It looked like a little Jimmy Somerville in denial about his hair loss, or Bobby Charlton in the 1966 World Cup final. It was only when I realised that I'd be sharing communal showers after my five-a-side soccer game that I began to panic. If my newly-shorn manhood was spotted in the gym, so what? I didn't know those people, but my twice-weekly game was attended by my friends, so there was no way I'd be up to the humiliation. I thought about it constantly and made up an excuse to not go on the Wednesday, but by the Saturday, I'd totally forgotten that I had shaved down there and stripped off. Before I even got into the showers my so-called friend pointed and laughed: 'Did you shave your bollocks?'

I replied instantly. 'Yeah, what about it?'

'For who?' he asked.

I thought about it and said, 'For me'. I've been a comic for twenty-two years and I've never evoked a laugh as hysterical, especially among men, as I did when telling them I shaved my pubic hair *for myself.*

'Ah, come on,' I barked back. 'You're saying none of ye have done it?'

'No,' they all replied.

That wasn't the worst thing, however. What nobody tells you is that it itches like hell when it grows back. Imagine having different grades of sandpaper in your underpants for several weeks. It was really scratchy. After one particularly warm day, I went home and just placed a plastic bag of ice on it for the afternoon. I had a genuine moment of clarity as I sat there. I thought to myself, I'm never going to meet anybody. There and then, at that moment, I knew that I was going to die a bachelor.

I had a gig that night and hobbled into the International Bar in Dublin. That night I would meet my wife for the first time. We exchanged phone numbers and I knew that she was the one. How romantic. I didn't play games. When I texted her, I said *I want to go on a date as soon as possible.*

She texted back … *Yes.* How romantic. However, I realised that I couldn't let anybody see me naked for another month at least. How stupid.

On our first date, in a city-centre pub, I was desperately trying not to scratch. For our second date, we went to the cinema and my seat and trousers were in a battle – it was excruciating. For our third date, which apparently is the get-it-on date, we just went for a meal and I said I had to go back home as I had an early morning. I hadn't had an early morning at that point in my life since my birth. Eventually my natural state re-emerged and the itching and scratching stopped. I haven't gone at it down there since, but have made my eyebrows my target instead. The reason? Because they are as untamed as the rest of my hair.

One mortgage and three kids later, I'll always remember my wife's astonished face, as she breathed, 'What have you done to your eyebrows?' Like down below, once you pluck, you are f##ked. At least nobody can see your pubic hair unless you're playing five-a-side. Instead of the scratching, my left eyebrow made me look like I was surprised all the time. As my mother said to me countless times growing up: 'Leave yourself alone.' What good advice. Now my wife says it too.

2. He had an STD that wasn't an STD, but he couldn't tell the difference.

This is another one that I thought Lorna didn't know about. Now, there is quite a lot about me that Lorna is aware of, being married to me. For a start, I don't like butter. I don't like milk either. For years, growing up, I'd never eat sandwiches at any event. My life was ruined by well-meaning mammies forcing ham sandwiches down my throat, saying, 'There's only a scrap of butter on it'. One of my first-ever memories was of my playschool teacher telling me to drink my milk. I tried and vomited it all over the sand pit. In Ireland there is butter on everything: you could buy an insurance policy and they will ask you, 'Do you want butter on that?'

I spent my teens a culinary outcast, afraid to ask the question that made every man, woman and child throw their eyes to heaven, 'Do you have anything without butter on it?' It was only when I went to college and got particularly sick after a meal that the resident nurse told me I was lactose intolerant. She explained to me that my serious wind problem and bowel issues all came from a reaction to lactose. For the first time in my life, I felt cool. I had 'an issue'. I have always been an issue but had never had an issue. When you're a pale-white red-haired Irishman, who was brought up by loving parents and never had any real problems, except for Leaving Cert maths, you just become the epitome of bland. But when I walked out of the Dundalk Institute of Technology students' nurse office in 1997, I had 'an issue'.

I started to daydream about where I'd slip it into conversations. I imagined myself at a posh party – women in evening gowns, men in monkey suits. A big silver tray with tiny hors d'oeuvres would be placed in front of me. I would ask politely, 'Do these contain butter?' The entire room and the string quartet would suddenly stop and gasp and I would lift my martini to my lips, take a sip and quietly say, 'Because I'm … lactose intolerant'. Two women would instantly be brushing my shoulder and saying in quasi-French accents, 'Ohhh, please, Bernard, tell us more.' Instead, it just resulted in years of me misreading food labels and numerous dashes to the nearest public toilet. Too many times I've been in petrol station queues, praying that they would just give me the key for the loos and not ask me to buy petrol. Lactose intolerance is very simple: when lactose goes in, it will come out, any time, any place and anywhere.

I thought my 'issue' would be just the edge I needed, enough to make me cock of the walk at Dundalk IT. Unfortunately, it was another intolerance, one that quite literally brewed its head, that made my name.

I was obsessed with the guitar when I was in secondary school. I used to sleep with it. This meant that by the time I got to college, it was the only thing I'd slept with. But then I found an amazing substance that actually gave me the confidence to talk to females … alcohol. I quickly realised that not alone was it tasty, it gave me a new personality. My life was soon focused on one thing: Thursday night. That was our going-out night in college. My catchphrase, however, became 'I drank the rent.' Piled onto this conundrum came another intolerance, this one much harder to fathom.

Around three months after I was anointed by the college nurse with lactose intolerance, I developed a burning sensation when I needed to pee. What started as a mild ember developed within a few days into a fiery blast. I also noticed an unusual liquid coming out of a place from where it had never come out before. Any normal young man would go straight to a doctor. I was not any normal young man and I didn't have any money for a doctor, so I did the only thing that would, I thought, help my cause: I told all my friends in the pub. They laughed, but assured me my secret was safe.

Later that evening, I got up to go to the toilet and one of them even said, 'good luck', but when I came back from my fire-peeing session, they were all standing on stools pointing and singing 'STD, STD, STD'. Everybody in the pub now knew there was something wrong with my penis. I wanted to kill them all. I wanted to go home to live in my room, never to be seen again. I was now the red-haired fella who had an STD. But then something unusual occurred in the pub. Lads started to slap me on the back and say stuff like 'Who is she?' What did they mean by 'she'? Then it dawned on me: STD. Sexually transmitted disease. I had a sexually transmitted disease. There was only one problem, though … the sexual bit.

To this day I do not know why, but I turned to my friends and said, 'But I've never had sex.' There was an actual pause in the whole pub and then an atomic explosion of laughter. I went from being a man with life experience to a boy with his willy on fire. Why hadn't I just kept it to myself?

The next day I went to the nurse again. She explained to me, at least three times, that I didn't have an STD, as I wasn't 'sexually active'. She kept saying it: 'sexually active'. What did that even mean? I was eighteen. I was active. I was sexual. I just wasn't sexually active with anybody else. Eventually she snarled, 'It's a yeast infection. You'll have to stop drinking beer.' Now, I didn't mind giving up choc ices, but beer? No way.

By the time I had left her dispensary, the entire planet had found out. That evening, when I was walking back to my house, the young lads who would normally sing, 'Get back in your biscuit tin, Ginger, Ginger' – their usual mode of greeting – were pointing at me and chanting in thick Dundalk accents, 'You're pissing fire, you're pissing fire.' How did they know? Of course, my housemates thought it would be hilarious to tell them. I stuck my head in the pillow in my room and thought about packing up my stuff and going home.

For the next week, I was a walking punchbag. Even people I didn't know were laughing at me. The yeast infection was going away, but the shame wasn't. But unknown to me, I gained the world's best superpower: I was intolerant to milk and yeast, but I actually grew tolerant to people laughing at me. I even grew to like it. I started telling the story to people and I didn't care about their response. Who was this guy? Until then, I'd never told funny stories about myself, but now I openly told people, 'I'm the only virgin in Ireland who's got an STD.' It was the first thing I learned in comedy: get the laugh, even if it's at your own expense.

When I was telling my story on stage for the first time, I could see first years actually looking at each other and laughing and pointing – clearly, I was not the first person this has happened to and I won't be the last. Pissing fire is never going to be a Disney moment, but if you're going to get a yeast infection in your willy, you've got to make the best of it. I learned a valuable lesson that I will pass on to my sons if they decide to go to college. If you find yourself pissing fire, for God's sake don't tell your friends in the pub – call me.

3. He faked a sixty-words-a-minute typing skill to get a job he didn't want.

When I met Lorna, I was an aspiring stand-up comedian, so even if I was broke, I had at least embarked on a career path of sorts, the culmination of several years of alternating hope and despair. Let's start with hope. When I was in school, I was in a band and thought I was going to be a rock star. I was obsessed with the Beatles. I wanted to be a red-haired John Lennon. While everybody else was wearing Naf Naf jackets and fighting over who was better, Blur or Oasis, I was busy trying to cut my own thick red Irish hair (see no. 1 on Lorna's list) into a mop top and asking my sisters to buy me black polo necks.

During my Leaving Cert year, I had no idea what course I wanted to study in college. I was never going to get enough points for medicine or law, as I was a very average student. I was also terrible at maths, and as passing the subject was a requirement to pass your Leaving Cert, the possibility of failing the whole thing was looming large for me. Eventually I found a course called cultural studies and, like thousands of people before me who had no idea what they wanted out of life and got high Cs in their exams, I jumped on board the good ship Humanities. In my case, it was at Dundalk IT, now called DkIT, for four years.

I loved every second of it, but finding a job afterwards was difficult for two reasons. First, the course was, like all humanities courses, brilliant but vague, so vague I had actually written a cultural analysis of vagueness in the Irish job market of 2001 as my thesis. Second, I was extremely lazy. In hindsight, I was suffering from what I've coined PPCL: Post-Partying and College Life. I found adapting to real life and actually working for a living so difficult after college that I contemplated staying there for ever. Instead, I found myself spending the next five years working as a barman, playing Irish music, which I'd learned gigging with my dad, and trying to get stand-up gigs wherever I could.

I was such a bad barman. I routinely forgot people's orders and could never work the till properly. But my biggest issue was that I never liked the customers, and that's really important when you're serving them food and drink. The pub was in Dublin city centre and tourists would ask me questions like 'Do you have Guinness?' In my head, I'd be thinking, you have come to Dublin, Ireland. You're in a pub and you are asking me, 'Do you have Guinness?' I would reply, 'Let me check,' and shout across the bar: '*DO WE HAVE GUINNESS?*' I'd answer it myself and say, 'I think so.' Most tourists talk about the friendly Irish barman or -woman and how helpful they are. I was not that person. My waitering left a lot to be desired, too. I once accidentally spilled a piping-hot Irish stew on a German lady. Her husband got so angry he got me in a headlock. When he eventually let me go, I composed myself and said, 'Is there anything else you would like instead?' I was just not suited to the service industry. Or, it transpired, to most other industries.

I worked on a building site for two days. The lure of the money was so big that even a self-confessed lazophile like me donned the yellow hi-vis and became a day labourer. I was told to go home when my foreman saw I wasn't able to lift a wheelbarrow of cement. He was also genuinely worried about the safety of his crew after I tripped out the entire building site's electrics when I let go of a bucket of water directly over a fuse box. I'd been trying to bring it up a step ladder and while accidents can happen, I hadn't seen the steps in the scaffolding. In essence, as they would say at home, I was useless.

However, I was, and still am, the world's worst interviewee. Harvard should have studied me as an example of what not to do or say when looking for a job. I've had a litany of disastrous job interviews. My most memorable by far was in 2002, for the tourist board of a certain Mediterranean island nation.

I was shocked when I got the interview, but then I realised that I had lied extensively on my CV. If I was being truthful when I was 23, my CV should have read like this:

Name: Bernard O'Shea

Address: Bedsit on Dorset Street, Dublin

Age: 23

Education: very average Leaving Cert in real subjects, but I got a 2:1 in Cultural Studies, so ask me anything you want about post-modernism, but nothing else.

Work Experience: very little. I worked on a farm growing up, but was mostly given painting jobs as under my watch, the animals

15

kept escaping, or worse. Worked in pubs in Dundalk and Dublin, but I hated the customers and was told regularly by my bosses and customers that I wasn't suited to it. I'm currently a night porter in a hotel, but I won't be for long, as I forget to do most of the duties, like wake-up calls and serving breakfast. I did two days on a building site but due to an accident filling a kettle with a bucket of water, that was it.

Hobbies: watching telly and drinking cans. I like to play my guitar, but only if I'm playing something I like. I play Irish music for money. It's okay … I suppose. I've started doing stand-up comedy. I'm not great at it, but like me most of the people involved in it love their pints, so I'll probably stick at it.

Other Interests / Achievements: nope.

However, the CV I actually sent out to prospective employers read:

Name: Bernard O'Shea

Address: Studio Apartment 2 (A), 46 Eccles Street, Dublin 1.

Date of Birth: 25 March 1979

Education:
Leaving Certificate: Heywood CS, Co. Laois
Nat. Dip. Cultural Studies
BA Cultural Studies, Dundalk Institute of Technology, grade 2:1

Work Experience:

1994–1997: Technical Agricultural Assistant, Co. Laois

This involved managing the day-to-day operations of a diverse agricultural operation.

1997–2000: Assistant Food and Beverage Operator, Dublin and Dundalk

My duties included maintaining sufficient bar supplies and allocating orders to customers.

2000–present: Senior Night Manager, X Hotel

Duties: managing staff (myself), controlling orders of stock, security.

Hobbies:

I enjoy volunteering with local charities. I also play Irish music and have a love of and passion for Irish culture. I also enjoy public speaking and stand-up comedy and integrating it into my work and social life. I'm also an avid reader and enjoy hiking and water sports.

Other Interests/Achievements:

I have a keen interest in *(insert whatever the job application is looking for here)*. Also, I'm currently furthering my education into the field of *(insert whatever the job application is looking for here)*. I also love travel and have been a frequent visitor to *(insert whatever country the company is from here)*. I have several awards for Irish music *(total lie)* and have been involved in several humanitarian campaigns *(total lie)*. I also enjoy the arts, particularly the visual arts *(be sure to put this in if the interviewers are continental: they will always ask you about it)*. I can touch type 60 words a minute *(never typed a word in my life – I actually hand-wrote my thesis and got my sister to type it for me)*.

With ten euros' worth of big brown envelopes and stamps, I posted hundreds of these CVs to employers who hopefully wouldn't smell the bullshite. Most did, but some got back to me, in hindsight not because they believed my CV, but because Ireland was going through a massive economic boom and nearly everyone was employable … *nearly* everyone. And with that came a request that I interview for the aforementioned tourist board of a certain Mediterranean island nation.

I borrowed a suit from a friend and took a tie from my father's wardrobe. None of it fitted, not even the tie. On the morning of the interview, I prepared by staying out until 4 a.m. and woke up with only thirty minutes to get across the city. I realised, for the first time in years, that I didn't own any proper shoes: even I knew I couldn't wear a suit with my Adidas runners. I had a brainwave. I could buy a pair of shoes on the way. Even though it would take me at least 45 minutes to walk across the city, I still thought I would have time to buy shoes on the way.

I ran out of the bedsit and onto the street. Luckily, due to the two hospitals in the area, there were plenty of taxis on the busy street. I flagged one down.

'Where to, son?'

'Leeson Street, please. Ooh, I'll need to buy shoes on the way.'

He actually stopped the taxi and looked me in the eye. 'Are you a bogey?' (A 'bogey' is Dublin slang for a messer, or a person of ill-repute.)

'No, I'm going for an interview and I don't have any shoes.'

He drove on. 'You know, I've seen a lot of things in this car, but no one has ever told me to stop at a shoe shop.'

I ran into a shoe shop on Talbot Street and headed to the counter, where a young girl was arranging shoes on a bargain rail. I had no time to spare. 'A pair of size nine black shoes please, for under forty euros.'

She took one look at me and I'm pretty sure she pressed the panic button under the till. 'We've nothing really under forty euros.'

I panicked. 'Anything brown, even?'

She looked at the rail and said, 'These slip-ons are size eleven and they are brown. They're thirty euros.'

With speed in mind, I bought them.

I ran out of the shop, climbed back into the taxi and slammed the door. 'Got them.' The taxi driver, whose name, I learned, was Dan, took off. It was like the shittiest ever version of the *Bourne Ultimatum*.

Unbelievably, I got to my interview on time. I paid Dan and then put on my new shoes. Three steps led to the Georgian door of the building. I'm good at climbing steps – mountains I find difficult, rock faces very hard, but I've rarely had a difficulty with small steps.

I landed straight on my face. The shoes were so big on me that I overshot the first step. I cut a gash on my forehead and, possibly due to the amount of alcohol I had consumed the night before, blood started to pump out from the top of my eye. At this stage, most people would give up, but not me. Then, as now, I was so full of self-delusion about my capabilities that I managed to climb the rest of the steps and ring the doorbell.

I was led into a grand Georgian hallway and the receptionist went and got me a tissue for my eye.

'They're running around half an hour late; I hope that's okay?' she said.

'Okay.' F##kin' fabulous, I thought. Still, I had time to stop the bleeding from my gash and stuff my shoes with toilet paper to make them fit and even wash my face – surely this is what everybody does while waiting for an interview? All of a sudden, things were looking halfway up.

I was called into a massive room, where a young man my age and an older man, around mid-sixties, were sitting at a table. Now, first impressions last, but I didn't know this or care at the time. For some reason, before I even shook hands or observed any formalities, I said, 'You have lovely toilets.' Eventually, the older man asked me to sit down. They started going through my CV and the first question the younger guy asked me was 'What exactly is a Technical Agricultural Assistant?

Eager to impress, I replied instantly, 'A farm worker'. D'oh. He then walked me through my CV, like a Mafia boss strutting his way through the back corridor of a Las Vegas hotel, tearing open every lie and getting to the rotting carcass of the truth. 'You don't have much office experience, Bernard.'

'Well.' I struggled to think of something in reply, but he did a 360-degree-turn and happily announced, 'But … you can type sixty words a minute. That's professional standard and that's what we're looking for here. We need an assistant to Mr ——— here with correspondence and possibly emails. We're also looking into putting some of our archive onto floppy disk (the height of technology at the time) and it would require massive amounts of [those words I'd heard so often since leaving college] DATA ENTRY.'

Oh shit. That's why I got the interview; because I said I could type. Here's the thing. I can't type. Even now, as I'm typing this story nearly twenty years later, I can't type. I use the two middle fingers on each hand. When I catch my reflection in the screen, I look like a highly caffeinated meerkat. However, in 2001/2, we were at the dawn of the digital revolution and every office in the world thought that paper would become a thing of the past. Every company wanted to shift all its information onto disk. Not online, because this was in the pre-cloud era, just disk.

The interview concluded and I was relieved. I thought to myself, if I get out of here, surely I could learn to type within a week or so. I shook their hands and went to head out the door. Then the younger guy said, 'Eh, Bernard, before you leave, we just need to see you type.' I had two options: say no and leave, or stay and type. To type or not to type, that is the question.

I could not believe the word that came out of my mouth: 'Okay.' I sat down at the leather and wood desk in front of an old-style PC, a big grey box that took up half the table. 'It's in Word now, Bernard,' he explained.

'Okay,' I stuttered, as if that made any difference to me.

He started to read a mock letter. 'Okay, so if you take this down, "Dear Sir …"'

I had two options. A: Pretend I could type and when it was over 'accidentally' delete the document; or B: Use my two-finger technique. I chose the two-finger technique and for some reason, even though he could see what I was doing, the guy read the whole letter out. It was the most embarrassing twenty-two minutes of my life. Halfway through, I was thinking, why won't he stop? He's only giving me self-belief. Had these men ever seen anyone type properly in their lives?

When the pain ended, he asked me to save it, which I had no idea how to do. As I got up to walk out, in complete silence, the older man asked his first and only question. 'Is there anything, Ber-er-nard, you feel you could bring to this job?'

I looked at him knowingly and said, 'My lunch.' He smiled and I left.

Years later, I used that line in a stand-up routine. Nobody believes that it actually happened, but it did.

Another half a year lumbered on and I was well and truly depressed. When people asked me what I did, the answer was the same as it had been six months before. Eventually, I had a eureka moment. Why did I need a job? I could declare myself something instead. On Thursday 14 November 2002, after a good feed of potato waffles and four cans of cider, I decided to become a playwright. I decided on being a playwright for five reasons:

* You can easily bluff it. Not a lot of people care about theatre, especially new theatre. There is a hard core of theatre lovers in Ireland, but I could just avoid them.
* I had actually studied theatre. If I got into a conversation about it, I could waffle my way through it, quoting Beckett if need be.
* You needed no evidence of your efforts. Unlike a writer, nobody would ask to see your play. I could tell them that we were in rehearsal or 'We're currently looking for a theatre brave enough to put it on.'
* I already lived the bohemian lifestyle by being penniless, so it suited me perfectly.
* I owned several scarves.

But before I did anything ridiculous, like write a play, I needed a new name. Bernard isn't the sexiest name. You never see male leads called Bernard in films. You never see women scream, '*OH, BERNARD, yes, yes, yes!*' on the silver screen. Bernard is the name of the boy who gets left behind on school tours. 'Where's Bernard?' the teacher might say. Bernard is crying his little heart out in the Aillwee caves as he sees the red minibus his school came on pull off into the distance. However, the name Bernard has a good precedent in the theatre world. There's George Bernard Shaw and ... well, back then that was the only one I could think of. So I decided, in homage to him, that I'd call myself Bernard George Shea. Instantly, I felt like an artist who could easily survive on cigarettes and self-importance.

After about two weeks of telling nobody my thespian plan, I eventually got down to writing a play. I had never written a play before or even owned a word processor, so I borrowed an ancient laptop off my brother-in-law and set to work. My play was called *Waiting for the Death of a Bedsit*. It was a cringey title. I thought it was cool and irreverent and showed how intelligent I was.

Waiting for the Death of a Bedsit
A play by Bernard George Shea

A bedsit in north inner-city Dublin. A man is asleep in a bed. He wakes and sits up.

Bernard: What's the point in getting up? Nobody calls to see me any more and I've no food. I had a dog, but he left me and ran away to the pound. He promised when he got there that he would send for me. That was a year ago. Apparently, he told all the other dogs that he sent me to live with a lovely family on a nice farm. I used to have a girlfriend, but she left me for a civil servant. I found out she was cheating on me when I filled out a form in the office that he was working in. Three weeks later, they posted me out another form. I had to fill it in and send them back my P60 and P45. Three weeks later, they sent me out another form saying I hadn't completed the original form correctly. I also had to get my original birth cert and send that in to them. Six weeks later, they sent me out another letter, stating that I was correct: my girlfriend *was* having an affair with a civil servant. I was going to confront her, but I couldn't be arsed filling out the rest of the forms. I confronted him, though. I wanted to punch him in the face but then he told me I was due over two hundred euros back in a tax rebate, so I left with two new forms. But once that money comes in, I'm going to confront him. He said it should be another six to eight weeks and then I'm going to let him have it. Oh, I am going to let him have it. I have the 'Let him have it' form so, in another year and a half or so, they will regret it.

He gets out of the bed. He is wearing a pair of underpants and a T-shirt. He walks over to a sparse counter and puts the kettle on.

Bernard: I love a cup of tea in the morning. I also love eggs. I also love toast. I also love sausages. I also love black pudding. I also love bacon. I also love fried tomatoes. But you can't have them all.

The kettle boils and he breathes in the steam.

Bernard: Maybe someday I'll have tea bags. And then if I'm lucky … a cup.

There is a knock at the door. He runs out of the room. A man enters. It's the landlord.

[This is the most cringey element of my play. I also play the landlord.]

Landlord: Where are you? Come out, you fat lazy lump. You owe me two months' rent. I know you have it. I got a letter in the post from the civil servant your girlfriend was cheating on you with and you're due a tax rebate. You don't have a job. I know that. You won't get one either, because you're lazy. Lazy men are the parasites of progress and you are the tapeworm of prosperity. *I want my rent.* I will be back for it, mark my words. I will be because the audience can't keep looking at you for another forty-five minutes and you need to build suspense. Do you hear me? *You need to build suspense.*

The landlord leaves. Bernard re-enters the room.

Bernard: Phew, that was a close one.

This was the opening scene. That was all I wrote and it took me three months to write it. There were supposed to be forty pages in total. At the time, I thought I was the new Beckett, but I eventually decided to feck it. I didn't even look to see if there was a theatre to put it on. My lack of motivation to do anything except write excessively about my lack of motivation was all I was motivated to do. Even if I did finish it and find a theatre to put it on, I eventually realised I'd just copied *Waiting for Godot.*

I failed at becoming a playwright. Even worse, I failed at becoming something that I'd made up and didn't even have to do anything to be. You have no idea how low you can get when you realise you're not even good at doing nothing.

* * *

For me at the time, Dublin was a horrible place. Everybody was obsessed with property. I remember one night in a bar on Wexford Street, I asked a girl if she would like a drink and she said, 'Do you own or rent?' That's how caustic the first boom was. I wasn't on the boom bus and I was secretly jealous of those who drove nice cars and went on lavish holidays. But in the city centre, in the cracks of economic prosperity, lay a home in which myself and others like me found refuge. The

International Comedy Club on Wicklow Street. It's the home of Irish comedy, full stop, and myself and a few friends lived and breathed the place. I also spent most weeks' rent in it on Guinness or cider, but that didn't stop me liking it. The only problem arose when we left it to go elsewhere. Any time I got talking to a member of the opposite sex and told them I was a stand-up comedian, the constant rebuttal was 'But I've never heard of you.' Added to this, I had no money or prospects. I needed a job, but I needed one that didn't involve showing up in the mornings but at the same time made me seem important and cool.

One night, at a friend's house party, I realised that I was the only person in the room who was unemployed. House parties back then were an excuse to get absolutely plastered in someone else's house and save yourself a small fortune on pub prices. There was no effort in them. You would just show up at a rented house with a bag of cans and go in, whether or not you knew the people. When I think of the number of floors I slept on in Dublin at that time, waking up not knowing whose house it was or who anybody in it was ... It seems absurd now, but it was a regular weekend for me then. Now, when we invite people over, we just pray they leave at 7 p.m., so we can start bedtime.

At one such party I got talking to a really pretty Spanish girl called Amy. I've never been good at chatting women up, so much so that one of my friends used to say, 'This town is full of women Bernard has nearly shifted.' I just presumed she was talking to me to practise her English, or was waiting for her friend. It was odd when she asked me if I would like a drink. I told her that I had my bag of cans and that I was alright.

When she went to the toilet, my friend Neil said, 'She's trying to chat you up'. I couldn't believe it – a woman chatting ME up? When she came back, I tried desperately not to be myself. I asked what she did, and she told me that she was a doctor. *A doctor*. Jesus Christ, I had about €12 to my name and hadn't shaved in weeks and I was being chatted up by a sexy Spanish doctor. As the night went on, I was also impressed with her ability to talk about subjects that didn't include house prices or my career trajectory.

But when she eventually asked me, 'So, Bernard, what do you do?', I knew I couldn't say stand-up comedian or playwright. I knew if I told her the truth, and said that I struggled with doing nothing, I was out of the game. I drunkenly perused the room. Everybody had passed out or was too drunk to notice what I said. I realised that it was safe to swim into an ocean of lies. I cracked open another can and told her I was a … 'Writer, I'm a writer'.

She was excited. 'Oh my God, I always dreamed of being a writer.' She told me about her love affair with W.B. Yeats's writing and that that was why she had come to Ireland. We talked until the morning and I told her that I was writing my first novel, based on the Irish economic boom, and I was cleverly calling it *Boom*. It was based on the collapse of the then-booming Irish economy and how it was going to affect the 'bourgeoisie'. It was a satire – well, I thought it was.

'Maybe I could read your book?' she asked as she left with her drunken friend. We set a date for the following week. I told her I'd bring a few pages along.

I didn't sleep for the next few days. I had my first real commission. I had to write a satire on the Irish economy to impress a sexy Spanish doctor. Who needs advances from publishers when you're trying to impress a woman? For the first time I was truly motivated. I started it with a quote from W.B. Yeats, the only one that I remembered from my Leaving Cert English, which I adapted for the climate at the time, but which would unfortunately turn out to become a reality. I wrote it in three days.

* * *

'For men were born to pray and save:
Economic Ireland's dead and gone,
It's with Michael O'Leary on one of his planes.'

It was 7.30 in the morning and Marie had just woken up. She lifted her head above the crisp linen sheets she had bought from House of Fraser in Dundrum Town Centre just the previous week. Her mind sparkled into joyous rapture as she pondered, 'My God, what would we do without the Luas?' A tender voice echoed down the hallway: it was Fuinneoga, her beloved three-year-old son. He tripped just outside his Bear in the Big Blue House-decorated en-suite and began to cry. Marie loved her son, but there was no way she was putting down a carpet, as it was 'so 2001'.

Fuinneoga roared out: 'Mammy, I've hit my head.'

This incensed Marie, as she replied, 'In Oirish, Fuinneoga, okay? You're never going to learn if you keep speaking the Béarla.' She tumbled out of the four-poster bed that had been bought in Tuscany on her honeymoon with her husband, Jamie. It had taken seven weeks to ship over, but Jesus, it looked good, even if did clash with the post-modern feel of the rest of the house. It was a compromise she just had to make.

Bang! She knocked over the bowl of All-Bran she had placed on the Bauhaus-designed bed locker. It was her Sunday morning ritual, to have some fibre-based cereal as she digested the *Sunday*

Business Post. Jamie would normally reflect gently over the pages of the *Observer*, while munching like a placid elk on his corn flakes, which had been bought from Aldi, but tasted just as good! Jamie and Marie would often fight over the Sunday morning papers: their marriage had been on tenterhooks ever since Marie walked in on Jamie reading the *Sunday Independent*. He swore blind that he hadn't bought it himself and that there was nothing else to read while he was on the bog.

'How could you?' she cried. 'Please God, tell me you didn't read the *Life* magazine. Don't lie to me, Jamie.' She never did find out. It was just one of those little secrets that every marriage has to live with.

Marie pulled the blinds in the master bedroom. The light gushed in and bounced off Jamie's plasma screen TV. He always complained, 'Like the only f##king programme RTÉ broadcasts in high def is the news. Christ, like, how much of Anne Doyle can a man take?'

Suddenly Marie felt faint. She began to have a seizure in front of the plasma. Jamie tried to grab her before she hit the floorboards, but he was too late.

She can't remember much of what happened next, only a small house in the country. Rain outside. She looked around the room. She saw her entire family dressed in Flahavan's tracksuits. Her mother appeared warped and ghost-like.

'Would you like a cup of tea, Mary?'

'No, I'll have a latte, Mum.'

'A latte? What's that, Mary?'

'Where am I?'

'You're at home, dear. I have nothing for the tea, only some bread and ham, but there's a lovely apple tart in the fridge.'

Her brain began to melt.

'I don't say apple tart any more, Mum, it's apple pie. I don't buy bread and ham any more, Mum, either. I buy ciabatta and Parma ham slices.'

'Would you like a biscuit, Mary? Look, I buttered it.'

Then Marie saw a horrible vision of the Marietta-biscuit sandwich, butter oozing from the holes in the biscuit. Her father held her down, while a priest forced a three-litre bottle of Homestead fizzy orange down her neck.

'Our Lord Jesus Christ himself drank Homestead – "Brings Value Home/*Ag teacht chun tí*"'

As she strained to move her head, Marie caught sight of a copy of *Ireland's Own* on the kitchen table and *The Messenger* with 'Happy 1984' on the cover. Everything went dark.

She opened her eyes. Jamie was standing over her with the digital remote control in his hand.

'Are you okay, Marie? Christ, I knew we should have stopped buying cereal from Aldi. Something is happening, Marie, I can't quite make it out ... it's something to do with the economy. It's all over the fecking news.'

They sat rooted to the Ronseal-protected floorboards and stared at the manic RTÉ news reporter screaming like an epileptic seal into the microphone. In the background the Central Bank was on fire. The bus lanes were gradually disappearing. Every car was morphing into a rusty Renault 4. In the background, Temple Bar was evaporating and cappuccino ran through the streets like sacrificial lambs' blood. The skater kids were screaming like mental patients: 'Aggggggggghhh! Must ... sign on ... have to ... go on something called ... dole.' One of them was violently puking onto the street as her banana, ginger and strawberry smoothie turned into lukewarm milky tea.

News began to stream in from around the country as the reporter did his best to control himself.

'We're not quite sure yet what has actually happened here, Anne, but it seems like the economy is collapsing around us. Earlier reports today suggested that nearly half the country went to Mass and, afterwards, newsagents were stunned when copies of the *Irish Press* appeared from nowhere on the shelves with the front page headline declaring: "We told you this would happen, but you wouldn't listen to us." There have been several sightings of women wearing headscarves staring at statues of the Virgin Mary, while the Monasterevin bypass has completely disappeared. There are also unconfirmed sightings of people having picnics – yes, I repeat, picnics – just outside the Green Isle Hotel. The transport infrastructure, however, is completely the same. Back to you in the studio, Anne.'

It became clear to Marie that what she'd had was a vision. Jamie started to cry.

'I have a secret, Marie, and I think now is the time to tell you. You see, my name is not Jamie. It's ...' (he drew a deep breath) 'It's ... it's John Paul and I ...' (tears were now flowing from his eyes) 'And ... and I want to join the guards.'

Marie grabbed his hand.

'It's okay, Jamie, I mean John Paul. You see, my name is not Marie; it's Mary, yes, Mary, and I'm not an executive health management co-ordinator, I'm a ... nurse. There, I said it.'

John Paul screamed, 'I want to call Fuinneoga "Benedict" after the Pope. It will be okay, I promise, we can shorten it to Ben.'

A red light beamed from the Bang & Olufsen plasma, which was turning gradually into an old Bush television with a money box attached to the side of it, which only took fifty pence pieces. The newscaster spoke.

'We now go over to Dáil Éireann, where the Taoiseach will address the nation.'

The Taoiseach appeared in front of a blue/grey background. Looking tired and confused, he began:

'I wish to talk to you this evening about the state of the nation's affairs and the picture I have to paint is not, unfortunately, a very cheerful one. The figures which are just now becoming available to us show one thing very clearly. As a community we are living way beyond our means. We have been living at a rate which is simply not justified by the amount of goods and services we are producing. To make up the difference, we have been borrowing enormous amounts of money, borrowing at a rate which just cannot continue. A few simple figures will make this very clear ... we will just have to reorganise government spending so that you can only undertake those things you can afford. As we speak, the government is transferring all its debts into one large loan and transferring that loan onto a credit card we found in the Labour Party Press Office. I personally will do everything in my power to look as if I have everything under control. As I speak, my brother is trying to find the number of a man called "Paddy the Plasterer" – he's always good for a few quid. Until we meet again, good luck and, for God's sake, tighten your belts.'

Mary knew there was only one thing she could do. She started to make seventeen ham sandwiches and wrapped them in a Brennan's bread wrapper. She also made a flask of tea. Yes, tea ... horrible, non-herbal, non-Fairtrade, disgusting tea. Her eyes panned to John Paul, who was frantically trying to find the four iodine tablets that the government had posted out earlier in the year for just such an emergency.

They both knew where they had to go – the B&I ferry in Dún Laoghaire.

John Paul couldn't start the 4x4 and Mary's Nissan Micra had mutated into a box of USA assorted biscuits.

'We will just have to get the Luas, Mary,' said John Paul.

He faked a sixty-words-a-minute typing skill to get a job he didn't want.

Little did they know that, overnight, the Luas had turned into the entire cast of *Glenroe*. John Paul walked out onto Ailesbury Road. A horrific sight was laid before him. He squinted his eyes in disbelief. Parked on the footpath was a 2004 3-series BMW. Then, and only then, did he know that house prices had dropped. He fell to his knees and roared into the sky: 'Jesus Christ, make it turn into an 06 plate, please, oh Lord, I'll do anything.' But it was too late.

He heard the voices of his new neighbours. They were ... culchies.

'Jesus, shocking what's happening to the aul' economy, isn't it? We stopped outside the Green Isle Hotel for a picnic and there are thousands trying to get out of the country. Jesus, thank f##k I had a few bullocks: yer man that lived here swapped one of them for his house. Anyway, howya. Me name is Pádraig, sure now that we're neighbours you can call me Podge.'

The culchie went to shake hands but John Paul was crying like a schoolgirl.

'Suit yourself. We're f##king off anyway to Holyhead, sure I'll see you over there.'

John Paul knew what he had to do to save his family and earn some money. He looked deep into the culchie's eyes and said, 'Any chance of a start?' But the culchie had vanished. He had already secured a contract building refugee huts in Kilburn and was living in London under a false name, while also drawing the dole.

* * *

I thought I had written a cracker. I went down to a photocopying shop beside Trinity College and got four copies made. We had arranged to meet in a pub in the city centre that night. I was nervous but excited. In an unprecedented move, I even ironed a shirt. I was serious. I was ten minutes early to the snug in the Long Hall, waiting for my date.

Spanish Amy showed up and my heart was pounding, but she seemed a bit down. Eventually, she told me that she'd had such a long day in work and was shattered. She shared with me the details of her day and I nodded and sympathised as much as a human can possibly sympathise without suffering a neck seizure.

She saw that I was sitting on a few sheets and asked me, 'Oh, is that your book?'

'Well,' I said, 'it's a few pages – the opening chapter.'

She seemed genuinely excited. 'Can I read it?' She started to read it. I had to do a lot of explaining about what Ireland was like in the eighties and how far the country has moved on and developed.

'Do you know who would love this?' she said.

'Who?' I looked her in the eye, knowing that she liked me, knowing that I had accomplished something real: a connection.

She took a sip from her drink and said, 'My boyfriend.' She invited me over to dinner some night to her house 'to meet PJ. You would have so much in common. He's from the midlands too, and he's the same age as you.'

The only thing me and PJ had in common was her. I was so pissed off. I'd spent days trying to impress an attached lady. Eventually, though, lying in my bedsit watching telly and simultaneously cooking more potato waffles, I realised that even if it was a botched date, it had forced me to write. I was given an emotional deadline and it worked. All it took was the hope of a new romantic fantasy to get me to do a bit of work, and now, fifteen years later, another woman has been the inspiration to write an entire book. Thank you, Lorna. I

He faked a sixty-words-a-minute typing skill to get a job he didn't want.

love you. But please, please, please don't leave me, because I'm pretty sure that bedsit is gone.

4. He has dyed his hair blond and he thinks I'll leave him if he goes bald.

I'm a red-haired man. That makes me one of only three per cent of people in the whole world. My greenish-brown eyes put me in one per cent of all the humans on the planet. You'd think, being follically this rare, that I'd be a hit with the ladies. Nope. In fact, growing up in Ireland as a red-haired man puts you in the bottom three per cent of picks in the local disco. I'm also quite possibly the whitest man in the world. White Irish people look at me and think, 'Jesus, he's pale.' This means that a sun holiday for me is the equivalent of a claustrophobe going to the catacombs. Both will end in tears, alone, in a dark damp corner underground.

My first time in America was when I was on a J1 student visa. I was getting the subway to Grand Central Station. There was a baseball match on in Yankee Stadium and the crowds piled on. I gave an elderly African-American lady my seat and, as she sat down, she bellowed, 'MAN, YOU'RE SO WHITE. WHERE ARE YOU FROM, COWBOY?' I told her Ireland. She asked me what I was doing in New York in the middle of the summer. 'Boy, you are going to bake like an egg on a stone.' And boy was she right. I got sunstroke that summer.

However, other American ladies didn't mind my red hair and parchment skin. Some even liked it. This was astonishing for a twenty-year-old sunstroke-afflicted Irishman. Before I headed to America for the obligatory J1 work experience, I'd had a bad year with the ladies. Dundalk IT is in the border town of the same name, which has a reputation as a rough town, due to its proximity to Northern Ireland and, formerly, to the Troubles. When I left to go there, my mother gave me sterling, thinking it was in Northern Ireland. It's not. It's also where Ireland buys its fireworks. 'Be sure to mind yourself,' my mother would constantly say. 'Oh, and could you pick up forty Roman candles, two sky bombers and fifty sparklers for Mrs McCarthy's nephews?' It has plenty of shoe shops, chippers and barbers and loves 'the Town', Dundalk FC, its football club.

I lived for a year in a part of Dundalk called Seatown, which was extremely handy, as it was near the pubs where me and my housemates drank. Dundalk is the place where I had the best four years of my life as a student, but one horrific event was to diminish my confidence with the opposite sex for years.

I was in first year in college and had no experience with the opposite sex. And I mean none. To say I was a virgin would be unfair to virgins. I was a trier, though. I would do anything to please a woman who would even just hold my hand. On one of my first nights out, I ended up with a girl in a nightclub called The Ark, pronounced locally as 'D-Ark'. We were kissing and she asked me if I would like to go back to her house. I was so proud of myself. I wanted to thank her for even letting me be with her in public. (I didn't. I thought I could always send her a card the next day.) It was my first time ever leaving a nightclub while it was still on; normally I was left with all the other forgotten souls, peering into the bright fluorescent lights, being screamed at by bouncers, 'Have you no homes to go to?'

We got as far as the taxi rank just outside the courthouse. It was lit up by a string of strong outdoor lampposts. It was then that her demeanour changed. She squinted at me and said in her thick Dundalk drawl, 'Oh, yous hove red haoir.' It was only when she broke free of the disco lights that she could see my hair colour. 'Here, sorry, but no. I don't do gingours.' She doesn't do gingers? Just seeing somebody else's house would have done it for me, but don't tell me I might also have been getting real adult sex with a lady who found me attractive. As her taxi drove off, I decided, I'm dyeing my hair.

The next morning, I went to one of the three thousand barber shops Dundalk has to offer. I waited until I saw one that was empty and ran in. A man wearing a Celtic FC football top ushered me into the barber's seat. 'What can I do for you, son?'

I told him straight: 'I want to dye my hair.' He burst out laughing. He tried to ask me more questions, but every time he tried, he burst out laughing again. He actually held onto his heart and bent over the spare seat. Every time he looked at me, he spat more ridicule-laden saliva in my direction. I knew I'd gone to the wrong place.

Eventually, as he wiped the tears from his eyes, he said, 'You're in the wrong place here, sonny. You need to go to a haoirdrossor's' (hairdresser's).

A scrawny man holding a newspaper walked in. 'Well, Peadar,' the barber said.

'Well, Joe, just popped in to see what's the craic.' This was one of the guys who always hang around a barber shop. They talk to the barber and ignore the customer. I don't mind these guys normally, but I knew the second I left his shop, they would be pissing themselves laughing at the ginger fella who wanted to dye his hair.

I left the barber shop and walked into the first hairdresser's I found, near the main street in Dundalk. I was eighteen and had never been in a hairdresser's since I was about seven, when my mam would tag me along for a haircut when she got hers done. The minute I walked in, I knew it was a mistake. All the women looked like models, like the wives and girlfriends of men who owned cars and who had jobs, not of a penniless student who'd only left home three months before.

'Are you okay there?' said a really pretty girl wearing large hooped earrings.

It was then I had one of my first out-of-body experiences. I should have said, 'I'm grand, thanks. I was about to make a total f##king eejit out of myself by asking you to dye my hair blonde, but I won't now, thank you. Goodbye.' Instead, I watched myself walk up to her and say, 'I want to see if I can get my hair dyed blond.'

She told me to wait and went and got her manager. The woman appeared almost as if she had stepped off the floor of a music video. 'Is this the guy here?' she said. The receptionist said I was, and she walked over to me. 'You want to dye your hair blond?'

I actually gulped. 'Yeah.'

Instead of bursting into to tears of laughter, she said something worse: 'Why?'

'Why? Eh, I just do.'

'But you have lovely hair, doesn't he, Martina?'

Martina, the really pretty receptionist, unconvincingly muttered, 'Ah, yeah.' Great. So not only does Martina find me unattractive, but now the manager of the shop is mothering me. In hindsight, she was being incredibly nice, but when you're eighteen and a virgin standing in a hairdressing salon in Dundalk in the mid-nineties, knowingly making a f##king eejit out of yourself, you just want to run.

She went on, 'Did something happen in school?'

School! Oh Christ, she thinks I'm still at school!

'No,' I said, 'I was just enquiring.'

Another woman appeared. 'Your hair colour is lovely, son, there's women in here who look for that colour all the time.' Oh Jesus, another one. Now there were three of them. The third one unknowingly pointed out the problem: women want red hair, they just don't want to have sex with it. My visit turned into the equivalent of a teenager trying to buy condoms at the chemist and when they bring them up to the checkout, the shop assistant uses the PA system to call a price-check on them. Not that I needed condoms.

Then the manager told me that her daughter had married a red-haired man. She was basically telling me, 'It can happen. Ginger men can get married.' I knew from my scant knowledge of the Geneva Convention that this was allowed, but it was nice of her to remind me. They were all being incredibly nice, but I just wanted the ground to open up and swallow me. Then the manager said, 'I don't want you to leave here and put bleach in your hair, do you hear me, because that doesn't work.'

Eureka! I knew that hydrogen peroxide was in bleach and that it was used to make bombs, so ... blond bombshell. Ah, bleach, I thought. I need to get my hands on bleach. This was in the days before the internet, so I was very proud of myself working this out. She had barely finished her sentence when I was in a supermarket perusing the bleach section. I picked up the cheapest bottle I could find. Not alone was I going to have blond hair: soon, I would also be able to eliminate germs 24 hours a day.

My friend had rented a house near the town centre, so I called around and asked him if I could use their shower. Being a student house, there was no hot water, but I didn't care. I just wanted to kiss girls in daylight. It was February, though, and the shower was freezing. I didn't know what to do with the bleach and wasn't asking for any advice as it would start another embarrassing slag fest among my friends. So I started rubbing the bleach into my hair. At first it was okay, and then … heat … then … extreme heat and finally, my head was on fire. I ran the shower and got in. The combination of cold water and extreme heat was horrific, but the worst was yet to come. Bleach can blind you. My eyes started stinging so badly that I called my friend for help, but he had gone out. The burning was so bad I couldn't open my eyes. I stayed under the shower until the burning stopped, which was about an hour. Being a student house, there were no towels, so I dried myself with the jumper I was wearing. The irony of it all was that I still couldn't open my eyes as the stinging was so bad. Eventually that evening I could open them.

My hair had turned … red. It hadn't changed colour at all. Then I noticed all my pubic hair and my left eyebrow weren't blond, but white. White, as in the colour of white paper. Not off-white, but whitewash white. I couldn't leave the house. I did the only thing any self-respecting eighteen-year-old would do. I shaved off my left eyebrow. There I was, walking down the Dublin road in Dundalk, looking like one half of the Mona Lisa, while my skin was burning so badly that I had to stop every so often and let the cold air bring down my temperature. When my friends saw me, they thought nothing of it, as we regularly shaved each other's eyebrows off when we fell asleep after a night out. Who knew jackass adolescent behaviour could cover up my blushes so perfectly?

Twenty years later, I was doing a stand-up comedy gig in Dundalk. It was February and it was freezing. For nostalgia's sake, I walked from my old digs to the college and then into town. I stopped outside the hairdresser's and looked in. There was no eighteen-year-old virgin looking to get his hair dyed. I walked to the house where I'd showered in the freezing cold water. It had been renovated and it looked like it was occupied by a family who probably washed in hot water. It struck me that what had happened to me could never happen again. It's so simple now to find out whatever you want on a mobile phone. I think teenagers are much more comfortable with themselves and their image anyway, even if there's a lot of image bombardment for them to deal with. However, I felt happy that none of them would set themselves on fire while trying to dye their hair blond.

I started to walk back to my car. I really wanted to see a young red-haired man holding hands with a girl. It would have beautifully capped off my little journey down memory lane. But instead, as I walked past the taxi rank where I was so brutally let down all those years ago, I saw that somebody had sprayed a giant penis on the ground with 'Cum on the town' underneath it. It wasn't a beautiful moment, but it was a very Dundalk one. All I needed was for six or seven kids to shout, 'Get back in your biscuit tin, Ginger,' and my day would have been made.

Now, instead of trying to get rid of my red hair, I'm trying desperately to hold on to it. My mid-life or quarter-life crisis has become my wife's favourite plaything, replacing her old routine of asking me why I was in the toilet for half an hour on my phone – she never insinuates that I might be looking at porn, because she knows I'm looking at sports cars or attic conversions. 'Because I can't get any peace and quiet' would be my reply.

My recent journey in trying to keep my hair on my head has her constantly laughing to herself. She is taking acute pleasure in my physical collapse. While she achieves the remarkable feat of creating new humans with her body, my hair seems to be going the other way. Let me explain.

Whatever about the colour, I used to have loads of it. I could have hidden birds' nests and bin Laden in it, and no one would have found them. I would pride myself on how quickly it grew. It was only when I saw the top of my head as shot from a camera crane that I realised I was harbouring a bald spot. Now, not everybody realises they're going bald because of a camera thirty feet in the air. Allow me to clarify.

I was participating in *Dancing with the Stars*. I use the word 'participating' because I found out on live television that I couldn't dance, so, winning was out of the question. I also found out that my big belly looked like Moby Dick's bigger cousin. It didn't help that my dance partner was a perfectly proportioned petite woman of whom my wife would constantly say, 'She's so beautiful.' This while watching me trying to do a salsa or, as I called it, 'not have a heart attack on RTÉ 1'.

On my final night (the night I got eliminated), dressed as a human cat trying to dance a waltz (I think) I noticed from an aerial shot that a little bald patch had surfaced. I never thought I was a vain person. Yes, I'm stubborn and sometimes difficult; maybe I have a teeny tiny temper, but vain?

I was mortified. It was the first time in my life I felt I was getting old. I know baldness and age don't necessarily go hand in hand, but my hair? No, please God, don't take this away from me. It was bad enough to be talking to the press about my elimination while dressed as a cat, but one with a receding hairline! It was my taxi rank moment all over again.

I had to do something about it. I sat down the next morning and googled 'men's hair loss'. I got thousands of results, mostly based on scant science and hope. Remedies ranged from bull sperm to my second favourite, ginger root. Apparently, people rub bull sperm into their hair to make it grow, and in Asia ginger root is rubbed into bald patches. It also said that the number one and two reasons for baldness were stress and genetics. It couldn't be genetic, I knew. My father had a full hair of hair all his life.

I finally decided on getting a three-month supply of a common hair-loss tablet and a well-known hair-thickening shampoo and conditioner. I followed the consumption and washing/conditioning routines religiously for three months. There was one unusual result. Did the hair on my head grow back? No. Did my remaining hair grow luscious and thick? No. Did I grow a bizarre amount of pubic hair all over my body? Yes. I looked like a red-haired yeti. It got so bad that I actually had to go into a barber shop and ask them to do my ears and neck. I looked up the supplements I was taking and they were basically fish guts. The shampoo had some caffeine in it. If I'd known, I would just have eaten oysters and drunk more coffee.

It was the first time I felt ashamed of myself. I've made some bad decisions in life, had arguments with people that I shouldn't have, but I've always tried to fix them. When you, and you only, are the person involved spending silly money on vague promises, you can only stand back and think. I've always looked at hair-loss advertising on TV and thought, what poor f##king eejit is going to buy that? Me, that's who. My wife told me it wasn't my hair that was the issue, it was that I was afraid of growing old. No it's not. I'm not afraid of growing old, because I'm never going to get old. It was then I decided to get a hair transplant.

I thought a hair transplant would be simple. You go into a white room and they stick a futuristic helmet on your head and after thirty seconds you have a full head of hair. No. They basically implant new hair follicles into your scalp one at a time. It takes a while, too. Certainly not thirty seconds. More like a year. And there are needles, lots of them. This is a problem for me, because I hate needles. I want a quick fix to my hair-loss problem along with quick schemes for losing weight and earning more money. They say there are no quick fixes in life, only hard work, to which I say, 'What is science doing?' There can only be so many horrific viruses and erectile dysfunctions to cure. What are they doing about my hair?

My wife kept saying, 'Why are you so worried about going bald?' Because I've an odd-shaped head. My mother says it's because they had to use forceps to pull me out by the head. My sisters tell me it was because I was repeatedly dropped on my head as a child. Well, whatever the cause, I would not make a good bald man. What's the solution? I'm currently combing over to hide my scalpy desert, but it's only a short-term answer.

I've thought about all eventualities and it's basically come down to one thing. My wife. Essentially, like the girl who rejected me all those years ago, I couldn't let my wife leave me if I lost my hair. She keeps trying to reassure me, saying stuff like 'I'd only leave you if you cheated, or became a knife-wielding maniac,' but it doesn't matter. She took out the 'obey' part of the vows at our wedding. If I went bald and she wanted to leave, I could try and use her refusal of the oath to obey me against her. So I drew up an annex to our marriage vows and I left it out on the kitchen table for her to sign:

> I, Lorna MacNamara, who refuses to obey Bernard O'Shea, or take his name because I feel it's an antiquated tradition, hereby swear never to leave him if he loses his hair and has to go around with his odd-shaped head.
> Signed _____

She has yet to sign it.

My only conclusion is that my baldness is not caused by me. It's caused by stress. Stress that has accumulated over the last twenty years. Here are the people, places and things over time that have caused my baldness:

> Italian trains, honeymoons, Croatian holidays, Greek holidays, County Clare caravan holidays, Irish weather, all holidays organised with my wife, buses, nightclub bouncers, train station announcers, Italian rail strikes, buying a house, my wonderful beautiful children, Peppa Pig, my wonderful beautiful wife, all queues, coconut oil, veganism, all -isms, meetings of all types, mortgages, cars, bread and other people.

Let me start with my first holiday organised by my wife, because it set a precedent for all that followed.

PART TWO

Eejitry
in Relationships

5. He walked into a glass door on our first holiday and when I laughed about it, he got his revenge by playing on my fear of flying.

At the start of every relationship, it's exciting. You want to show your best side. Any little struggle your new partner finds themselves in, you want to be able to help them. When they are sick for the first time, you couldn't do more for them. You turn into Florence Nightingale on speed. The first time they have trouble in work, you assure them, 'It's them, not you.' This support finds its way into our marriage vows: for richer, for poorer; in sickness and in health ... It's easy to say these words, but a lot harder to keep them.

When does the support run out? Over time, I've noticed that 'support' from my wife dwindling, mostly due to my stupidity and my lack of support for her. Notice the word I'm beginning to hate: 'support'. It's bandied about by relationship experts as the secret elixir to cure all ills. In fact, the word they should hammer into you is 'Okay'. When your partner gives out to you for throwing out a blanket she had since birth because you thought it was dragged into the house by a rabid dog during a storm and was not an heirloom, instead of talking about it, just say 'Okay'. If your husband relentlessly harps on about why you don't clean out the fireplace and it's not his job, don't start a heartfelt conversation about helping each other, just say 'Okay'. That will stop arguments, until your partner cops on.

I know my wife doesn't listen to me any more. She puts on her 'listening eyes'. She looks at me with her head leaning to one side, looking like she's listening, but her brain and ears are far, far away. But how do you know when your partner, in the nicest possible way, doesn't really care if you get sick or hurt any more? Obviously, they still love and respect you, etc., but we have all been there when we felt and received what I like to call Love/Hate. For me the moment came when my wife started to talk about a friend of hers who was married to a 'fierce handy fella'. She began to mention other husbands who were so much better than me. When everything seemed okay, from nowhere this would land:

'Do you know Marie's husband? Well, he's very handy. Last week, she went to work and when she came back, he had put a two-storey extension on the house and had it furnished to her exact specifications. She was wrecked after work and he told her to sit down and he'd take the children and the baby for the night. He gets up to do all the night feeds and he has a full-time job. He's also running a marathon next week to highlight "lazy bollocks syndrome" in men.'

I don't mind, because I just tell my wife that husbands who are amazing with the kids, handy around the house, caring, fit and healthy are generally feeling guilty about the affairs they are having. There are no perfect people or relationships, but when the first cracks in the caring concealer appear, it can be an eye-opener in most relationships. I realised I was in a relationship with a normal person, who would pretend she didn't know me when I was in an embarrassing public situation, nearly twelve years ago when we first started going out.

Our first trip away together as a couple was to Berlin. I'd never been there before and neither had Lorna, so for my birthday, I booked the flights and the hotel. Lorna left it until we got to the airport to tell me that she was a nervous flyer. It was the start of the relationship, so I was genuinely considerate. I listened to her and tried my best to calm her down. I suggested we go for something to eat first and then that we browse in the newsagents before we headed down to the gate. She told me she had brought a book, but because I was Considerate Bernard, I was only trying to keep her mind off the flight for a long as possible.

When we got on the plane, I held her hand until we got into the seat. I even surprised myself when I told the air steward in our section that she was a nervous flyer. He was extremely kind and told me he would keep an eye on her. I took the in-flight brochure and magazine and started to talk rabidly about aftershave. 'Oh, look, honey, CK One is just twenty-four euros.' Anything to keep her mind off the take-off. I even asked the person sitting beside us if he could swap seats, so Lorna got the middle seat and didn't have to look out the window. I was playing a blinder. Considerate Bernard was acing this.

Then the pilot came on to make an announcement. His voice sounded like a cross between a well-serviced male lion and Barry White. 'Ladiesss and Gentlemeen, yooooour very welcome on board this flight from Dub …. lin to Ber …. lin. It will take just under two and a …. quarter hours. If we get a good headwind, which I hope we do, we could be in

Germany by let's say, ehhhh …. Just on the button of half-past three. We'll be heading out over Dublin Bay and we'll be cruising at around thirty-five thousand feet over Britain and the continent, so sit back and relax. Cabin crew to take-off positions pleeeeeeasohyeah.'

Why in God's name do pilots need to tell us what height we're cruising at? Never in my life have I seen a passenger exclaim, 'Actually, you should cruise over Luxembourg at thirty-seven thousand feet.' Passengers don't have a clue or care. You don't want to be reminded that you are seven miles up in the air inside a large metal tube, being propelled by what are basically two gigantic Bunsen burners and an overwhelming belief in the laws of physics. He would have been much better off saying, 'Sit back and imagine how sexy I look as I press the magic button that hands this baby over to Jesus, Mohammed and Buddha.' That most definitely would have taken Lorna's mind off the fact that she was on an aeroplane.

During take-off Lorna squeezed my hand tightly. I was there for her, and Considerate Bernard even combined it with a little cuddle and whispered into her ear, 'It will be fine. This is going to be a lovely flight.' I could not have been more wrong. I have never in my life been on a flight with more turbulence. It was like being in a tumble dryer with a set of golf clubs. I'm not a nervous flyer, but when you hear, 'We will not be serving any food or liquid for the duration of this flight,' you know it's going to be a bad one. Lorna was in a catatonic state. I was doing everything to calm her down. There were babies screaming, grown men weeping and several hundred cheese-and-ham toasted sandwiches going to waste in large metal boxes. I could smell them, along with the fear and the odd waft of urine. When we landed, she was so shaken up that I thought she was going to break into tears. I carried her bag and held her hand.

Now, I know what you're thinking. Is holding someone's hand such a massive thing? Well, it is for me. Let me explain. I've never been a touchy-feely person. I physically find touching someone, unless in a very pleasurable moment, very hot. Not 'hot' in a sexual sense, but in a physical one. I remember having to hold my partner's hand on outings in primary school and thinking, 'My hand is on fire.' My daughter is the same way. We both run hot. For us, holding on to someone else's hand for longer than three minutes is like holding on to a baked potato. Also, I feel that I can express my emotions by telling the person. My wife is a hugger. I'm not, never have been. I am also not a fan of PDAs, or public displays of affection. It drives my wife mental. It's just that I don't believe that displays of our physical feelings in front of strangers are important. I know that to my wife, it shows her that I love her and all that romantic stuff, etc. etc., but when I see young couples on holidays expressing their love by wearing the face off each other, I don't think, 'Oh, young love', I think, 'If your mother could see you do that now, she would beat the back of your head with a coal shovel.' It's possible that I don't like it because I'm a Catholic, bred in Ireland, who has only ever cried when we do well at international football tournaments, but PDAs just make me uncomfortable.

'You're afraid that somebody might see you,' my wife says. I won't lie, that is a major part of it, too. But will all those PDA merchants clean out a catheter for their partners in old age? Surely that is the most romantic PDA, but you won't see it near the Trevi Fountain or on the Champs-Élysées.

When we landed in Berlin, it was raining, so I left the bags with Lorna, asked her again if there was anything I could get her and ran out to the taxi rank. As I was running towards it, I saw one of the drivers put his hand out in a very bizarre 'stop' gesture, almost like he was one of the Spice Girls in the middle of a dance routine. He was animated and his eyes were piercing. As I continued running towards him, he started to wave his hands, like a six-year-old pretending to be a tree in a school play. What is this guy's problem? I thought.

And then, BANG. I ran into a glass window at full tilt. I hit it with such a thump that as I hit the ground, I could still hear the reverberations. I hit it so hard that my head was pounding and it took me nearly a minute to get up. When I did, eventually, stand up, I noticed two things: unlike when a migrating bird hits a window and dies, no one in Schönefeld Airport was crying at the loss of innocence. Instead, most people were either trying not to look at me or trying to hold back laughter. The taxi driver I'd been running towards wasn't even trying not to laugh; he was looking directly at me and guffawing with two other drivers.

But the second notable thing was that Lorna was nowhere to be seen. Where was my future wife, whom I'd helped so admirably on the plane journey? Why hadn't she come directly to my aid?

My phone rang. It was Lorna. 'I found a train that will bring us to the city centre.'

I was still dazed and in pain. 'Where are you?'

She paused and said, 'Oh, by the train stop … it's just down the stairs from where I left you off.'

Hold on a second: left me off? Then there was another gap and finally, the truth. What had happened was that the woman to whom I'd been so considerate during her terrible flight had seen me walk straight into a glass window, had seen everybody laugh at me and had made a split-second decision to bail and go to magically find a train. She spoke really quickly: 'You okay?'

I hung up. As I gathered my bags and headed to the train, I had a decision to make. Would I start our first-ever fight on our first-ever trip away, or would I pretend nothing had happened? When I met her at the train platform, she had been crying … crying laughing. 'I'm so sorry. I left because I didn't want to laugh at you in front of other people.' Here it was, delivered on a plate of embarrassment; she'd walked away from me because she was embarrassed by me. 'No, that's not true,' she said, but I knew that it was.

All that weekend she would, out of nowhere, just burst into laughter. I agree that watching someone absolutely poleaxe themselves off their own reflection in a glass window is hilarious, but not when it's you. When it's you, it's just painful and embarrassing. But I also knew that the initial charade and sheen of the relationship was over with. Instead of farting in front of her, I'd walked into a giant window in a German airport.

Sure, the start of relationships is fun, but when it gets into the nitty-gritty, that's when the game really starts. I call it playschooling. When you're small, you go to playschool. You play in the sandbox and take naps, and every now and then you learn about nature and words. Every child loves playschool, but then out of nowhere comes school. You can apply this to nearly every aspect of your life. Work, for example. You start off on your first day and you're shown around. You're introduced to accounts, who seem so friendly, then HR, then on to sales. Debbie from reception tells you to help yourself to tea and coffee. You think to yourself, this is such a nice, supportive place to work. Watch out, you're being playschooled. Two weeks later, you're in HR because you stole Debbie's milk and your dress code is not in keeping with the company ethic. That's what relationships do: they playschool us, but you don't learn as much. I learned that day that my wife will, from time to time, find me so embarrassing to be around she will, in effect, disown me. However, I feel comfortable in the knowledge that she didn't run away and she has stayed with me. Nobody's perfect – that's what we have said to each other from time immemorial.

So it was only right that I expressed my love for Lorna on the trip home by refusing to give her the middle seat. Instead, I told her the truth. 'I'm six foot two, I have to sit on the outside, that's why I always book the outside seat. I know you're nervous, but try to enjoy the view and I'll meet you in the taxi rank when we've landed in Dublin.' I also told her the truth about air travel, something she has reminded EVERYBODY we know about several times. When the plane took off, I wanted to deliver some realism to her fears. I didn't want some wishy-washy stuff that Considerate Bernard would say. Instead I looked her in the eyes and said, 'Don't be frightened, Lorna. If the plane crashes, we all die.'

In hindsight, it was a terrible thing to say to a nervous flyer, but she was so furious with me for saying it that she actually forgot how much of a nervous Nelly she was and concentrated all her negative emotions on to me. When we landed in Dublin, she looked at me and said, 'I've been thinking. I don't think we're a good couple because you're a bollocks.'

'Have you been thinking about that for the whole flight?'

'You're not worth a full two hours, Bernard, I read my book.'

I then declared, 'You're welcome, Lorna, I've cured you. You weren't nervous on the flight because I distracted you – the same way you got so distracted when I walked into a window that you rang me from a train station platform that you magically found in your distress.'

We walked silently towards the taxi rank. Luckily, I didn't walk into a window and, luckily, we went home together.

Now, ten years and three kids later, she still finds it hilarious to shout 'WATCH OUT' when I'm walking towards a sliding door. When we had to put new windows into our house, she rang me. 'Bernard, they left the old ones outside – be careful not to walk into them.' Or my favourite: 'Bernard, it's very hot in here. You wouldn't walk into, sorry, open, a window?'

I'm not a relationship expert. I'm not even good at being in relationships. In fact I'm not even sure what a proper relationship is, even though I'm in one, but I do know this: it's not what you find lovable about your partner, it's what you can put up with and, hopefully, after a few years, laugh about.

PS: Schönefeld Airport, your windows are too clean.

6. When we met, he couldn't do 'normal' things, like other people.

I wasn't good at 'adulting' when I first met my wife. There were three things I couldn't do. She called them Bernard's Holy Trinity. I couldn't drive, I didn't have a bank account and I couldn't swim. When I look back now, my wife hadn't great patience in showing me how to drive. We drove around a disused car park in an industrial estate in Athlone and, after five minutes, she said, 'I think you should get lessons.'

The bizarre thing is that I love cars. I always have. But I never needed one until I started commuting to work. The bane of most Irish people's lives is Irish public transport. Once an Irish person starts driving, he or she will never have to hear mumbled announcements like 'The train on platform four to Sligo is late because it's gotten a talking part in a small independent film.' I thanked God that I would never have to see another Bus Éireann bus and listen to its 'LUGGAGE DOORS OPERATE' automatic mantra ever again.

Buses in Ireland are a mixed bag. They stop in every town in the entire country, the drivers are mostly grumpy and they definitely have favourite passengers. I've spoken extensively to bus drivers (well, maybe at them) and asked why they always give the old ladies with the shopping bags on wheels all the perks. The worst thing I found out recently was that Irish buses *did* have toilets in them in the eighties and nineties, but it was only when we got an economy that the passengers got enough confidence to use them.

The town I grew up in, Durrow, Co. Laois, is halfway between Cork and Dublin and was used as the stop-off point for every bus. When I was growing up, you could get a bus to Cork or Dublin twice every hour. Then the motorway was built and the town was bypassed and now there are no buses. It's odd. Growing up, life revolved around my sisters getting the bus to Dublin every Sunday; now Dublin, even in traffic, is only an hour and a half in a car. Towns that were once famous for traffic – Monasterevin, Abbeyleix, Kildare – have now been bypassed. Rural buses are, however, very different from urban ones. Maybe it's me, but I still see public transport as an episode of *Thomas the Tank Engine and Friends*. Dublin buses are street smart and have names like the 16A, the 42B or, my favourite, '*As Seirbhís*', which took me years to figure out was the Irish for 'Out of Service'. When I went to Dublin first, I couldn't get my head around why they were called the 11B or 12A. Why weren't they called after their starting point and final destination, like buses down the country? It was like a secret urban code I couldn't figure out. It took me days to figure out how to get on a bus that crossed the city. I could have figured out the *Da Vinci Code* more quickly.

Before electronic cards for fares, like the Leap card, everyone had to pay the driver by putting the fare into a metal slot in a machine at the top of the bus. In the eighties, my sisters used to say, 'Thirty, please', put thirty pence into the metal box and get on. The thing is, I didn't know that 'thirty' was the price of the fare: I just thought it was some kind of Dublin-speak or code you said to the driver. Embarrassing for me: I got on Dublin Bus for nearly ten years and said, 'Thirty please' and went on long and short journeys with it. If anybody from Dublin Bus is reading this, I apologise and possibly owe you a few fares. My defence is, I'm just a bit thick.

Trains in Ireland are also unusual things. I used to get a train called the Enterprise from Dublin to Dundalk for college. There were peace talks going on at the time, but it seemed like every train I was on got delayed due to a 'bomb scare in Lurgan'. This was so frequent that on Fridays, when I would get the train into Dublin to work at the weekend, I was always late, due to a 'bomb scare in Lurgan'.

The one thing that Irish public transport does well is that it always makes sure you pay. If you're interrailing in Ireland, don't try to hop on a train or bus without paying. Why? Because that's our thing. Ireland was the Land of Saints and Scholars in the Middle Ages, the Island of Emigration and Song in more recent history, and now we have the reputation of the Island of People Who Will Always Try And Get Away With Not Paying For Public Transport Abroad. On mainland Europe, they trust in you to buy a ticket for the train. They trust that you will not get into the first-class carriage and pretend you are the CEO of Google, while wearing your Irish football jersey and an inflatable hat in the shape of a hammer. Every Irish person I know, rich or poor, has got on public transport abroad without paying for it. It is the remnants of us being the poor, smelly child of Europe. There's a deeply ingrained devilment in Irish people that they just hop on and go, 'F##k it, I'll just pretend I didn't know.' It is also nearly impossible to arrest hundreds of Irish people who are singing, playing music or doing an agitprop stage show while going to anything that we are involved in.

Irish people travel and when we travel in groups, we sing, drink and don't bother our holes paying. And we shouldn't, because we got it put into the Geneva Convention. If you read it very closely, you'll see just after Article 3:

> Persons taking no active part in the hostilities, including members of armed forces who have laid down their arms, and those placed 'hors de combat' by sickness, wounds, detention, or any other cause, shall in all circumstances be treated humanely. Also, Irish people don't have to pay for public transport on the continent because they're great craic (fun or good-humoured).

There is another way of getting around Ireland, though, and that is sticking your paw out and hoping for the best. The Americans call it 'hitching a ride'; we call it 'thumbing'. When I told my wife I used to 'thumb', she was horrified, but I did so only when I'd drunk my bus or train fare to Dublin or back to Dundalk, which was pretty regularly. I found out recently that it's technically illegal, which is probably sensible because I have had a few scares. Once I got picked up straightaway by a lorry driver, who took me as far as Drogheda. After four hours of standing in the rain, I started walking towards a village called Julianstown. Eventually a car stopped for me. I got in and immediately felt that this wasn't good. The driver was impeccably dressed and was holding a yellow lampshade. After a quarter of an hour, he broke the silence and asked me, 'Do you want to know why I'm holding this?'

I very assuredly said 'No.'

'Good,' he said, really pissed off that I didn't join his surreal game. After another few minutes, he said to me, 'Would you like to join me for tea in Balbriggan?'

It was one of those moments when your brain decides to take over. I undid my seatbelt and very loudly exclaimed, 'You can let me out here please.' In fairness, the big weirdo did, but it was dark and raining and I had to walk another five miles to Balbriggan. After begging a night bus driver to let me on his bus into Dublin city centre in exchange for going into a petrol station and getting him a Wispa, I eventually got to work nine hours later and nine hours late. That was a typical weekend in my teens and twenties.

When I told Lorna about this, she was horrified all over again. I thought to myself, I'd better not tell her that I slept in Bryant Park in New York for a week when I was a student, or got on the wrong plane in Dublin and went to Brussels instead of Sligo (yes, that actually happened), or accidentally left Dubai once and crossed the border into Yemen, or nearly sparked a diplomatic incident on the Irish border during the foot and mouth crisis in 2001, or drove somebody else's motorbike into a ditch, or accidentally freed over a hundred deer onto a motorway, or ordered ten thousand drills instead of ten when I was on my 'holidays' in America, or was nearly arrested for my aforementioned sin of eating corn flakes out of the box in a tree on New Year's Day, or had an 'accident' on a train to Westport and had to lock myself into the toilet for three hours. The list is endless. And none of it was fun. It was just a series of patching over mistakes and hoping everyone involved would forget.

So when I met Lorna and she realised I couldn't swim, pay bills or drive she found it hard to comprehend. Her constant question at the start of our relationship was 'When are you going to learn to drive?'

It was not without difficulty that I managed to get my licence. I did my test four times. The first time, I just outright failed. However, the second time was catastrophic. Have you ever heard stories about crazy things that happen to people on their driving tests? You have?! Well, they are all about me. On my second attempt I was driving over a motorway bridge. The examiner told me to take the first left. I did. Here's a top tip. When a driving examiner tells you to speed up and pull into the hard shoulder as quickly as possible … that's not good. That's what happened.

I couldn't understand why he gave me such a weird instruction. He looked at me and in a very official tone he said, 'I'm informing you now that you have driven the wrong way down a motorway.'

I was confused. 'You said take the first left.'

He took out a little book of road signs and pointed to one, replying very calmly, 'Do you know what this sign means?'

I looked at it. It was obvious. 'No entry', I quipped instantly.

'Well, you entered down a slipway against oncoming traffic.'

The sad thing was, as he was driving me back to the test centre, I still thought that maybe I might have passed.

The third time I did my test, an examiner was testing my examiner, so there were three people in the car. I failed on the clutch.

The fourth time was the strangest of all. On the morning of the test, I was adamant I was going to pass. The test was going fine until I was entering a roundabout, when a car drove over it. I had to brake hard and reverse in order to let another car miss it. When I was driving back, I knew I had failed. When the instructor said I had passed, I did the strangest thing. I actually started to cry. I hadn't cried in years.

He kindly said, 'You can stay there and get your stuff together, then just bring this paper to the front desk.' I was actually crying.

I phoned Lorna and she was freaked by my agitated behaviour. 'What's wrong?'

'Nothing. I was just calling to let you know ... ' I paused for dramatic effect. 'I passed.'

Her reply came slowly but sharply, 'I'm in work.'

Six years later, as she gave birth to our first child, she looked at me and said, 'You cried when you passed your driving test, but not on the birth of your daughter?' Unbelievably, I had the cop on not to reply, but it took a lot for me not to roar, 'IT TOOK ME FOUR GOES!'

* * *

The second in my Holy Trinity is bill paying. Before I met my wife, I still paid all my bills with cash. This was possible as I lived in a bedsit in the city centre and could actually walk to the HQ of any electricity, gas, banking or any other national or international institution. Besides, I only ever had one bill to pay: the electric. I had an ATM card so I'd just take money out of my account to pay the bill. I was getting by pretty much okay until the digital age forced me into getting a credit card and to go 'paperless' and 'online'. It was during one of these 'paperless/online' forced transmigrations that I said what my wife feels is the most stupid thing I've ever said to another human being. I disagree. I will explain.

Lorna was constantly bugging me to switch to a bill pay phone. She pointed out that I was putting way too much credit into my phone and that a customised bill would be less hassle and cheaper. So she took me by the hand (literally) and brought me into a phone shop. We sat down with an eager young man for a 'consultation'. I find the use of that word a little bit extravagant – unless you're going to tell me I need kidney stones removed, please use another word. I have always just nodded off when people start talking figures. This can be difficult when your wife is an accountant. It's just that they have always bored me to death. As for percentages, I've never fully understood them or how to do them. All I know is that as I tuned back into my 'consultation' I heard a twenty-year-old man ask me, 'What would you be talking to your mother about?'

At first, I was a bit taken aback. Then I was confused, then I was angry. What business was it to a little fart of a bigger fart what I was talking to my mother about?

I told him straight. 'That's none of your business.' Lorna looked at me as if I had just shot him in the face.

He said, 'It's just that I'd need to know to see what the best package would be.'

I was completely annoyed now. 'What difference does it make to you? Why would you want to know? You're completely overstepping the line here.'

Lorna squeezed my arm. 'What are you doing? Just answer him.'

'No, absolutely no way. Did you tell him what you talk to your mother about?'

She turned me around in my seat, in the same way you would with a toddler when they're bold, and said, 'He asked you WHAT WOULD YOU BE TALKING TO YOUR MOTHER *ON*, NOT ABOUT.'

I thought about it for a bit and then said, 'No he didn't.'

He interrupted. 'Eh, I did. I said, what would you be calling her *on*. Like, a landline or a mobile?' Before I got to say sorry to him Lorna had left. After signing a phone contract that lasted three thousand years and gave them first option on my organs, I met Lorna in the car. She hit me with the line 'You f##king eejit' and then something that I've heard from many different people: 'You just don't listen.'

I don't listen, this is true, but if I did listen all the time, nothing interesting would ever happen to me or the people I'm with. Listening is overrated. I am hopefully the first person to ever think this or to write it down, but it's true. When was the last time you had a crazy night out with a great listener? 'Maybe you should just listen more often,' I'm told. I would but it's soooooo boring.

Yes, if I was a better listener, I wouldn't have had to sleep in the aforementioned Bryant Park in New York for a week as a student, because I'd have heard when they told me that there was little to no accommodation; or got on the wrong plane and gone to Brussels instead of Sligo, because I'd have listened when they told me at the check-in desk that the gates had changed. Or accidentally left Dubai once and crossed the border into Yemen – the tour operator told me not to get on any buses without telling him, but I didn't hear him. Or nearly sparked a diplomatic incident on the Irish border during the foot and mouth crisis – I was warned not to take selfies beside any military installation. Or driven somebody else's motorbike into a ditch – I was told there were no brakes on it and not to drive it over 35 mph. Or accidentally freed over a hundred stags onto a motorway – I'd been told, while working on a mountain drilling wooden stakes into the ground, to make sure above everything else to always close the high gates near the motorway. Or ordered ten thousand drills instead of ten when I was on my 'holidays' in America working at a DIY store – I didn't listen to my boss. Or had an 'accident' on a train to Westport and had to lock myself into the toilet for three hours – I wouldn't listen to my friend and drank a bottle of Tia Maria and milk, even though I'm lactose intolerant.

I would never have accomplished these fantastic feats of phenomenal stupidity if I'd LISTENED. So, here's my little philosophical entry into the well-being charts for the confused times we live in: *Stop listening and make mistakes.* It won't take off as quickly as mindfulness or yoga, but it is so much fun. So get out there and shit your pants on a train – just make sure you have a spare pair of trousers.

* * *

The third thing I couldn't do when I met Lorna was swim. Lorna found this amazing: 'But did you not learn in primary school?' Well, we were brought to the swimming pool, but I just used to hold on for dear life or take one massive breath and try and walk across the floor from one side of the pool to the other. When I turned thirty, I decided that no matter how much chlorine I had to swallow, I was going to learn how to swim. I went to group lessons, but guess what? I found it hard to listen to the instructor all the time. Then I went to one-to-one lessons but kept talking to the instructor, and then eventually I did both, and somewhere along the line I learned how to swim.

I was delighted with myself. Now I understood why hotels with pools were so popular and I couldn't wait to show the world my pale flabby Gaelic body on our next holiday. For our first 'sun holiday' together, Lorna and I decided to go to Lake Garda. Lake Garda is where the Irish gardaí go on their holidays (only Irish people will get this terrible joke).

When we landed in Italy there was a bus and train strike, which only added to the Italian-ness of our holiday. With no public transport available, we shared a taxi from the airport with another Irish couple. For some reason we tried to make holiday friends with them. We didn't realise we were doing it, but in hindsight, we were. However, they didn't want to make friends with us. To the point that, when I asked them where they were staying, they said, 'In a hotel.' When the taxi dropped them off, we berated them. They had broken an Irish law: being really friendly and having the craic to your face while never, ever wanting to see you again. We debated that they were having an affair, because who wouldn't want to get to know us? It's a peculiar thing, 'holiday friends'; you never know if the other couple like you or if they are just being polite. But why make holiday friends in the first place? Is the company of my wife not enough to sustain our relationship for a few days away together? Then again, I would find myself extremely annoying, but I'd talk to Lorna.

Checking in, the receptionist was possibly the rudest person I have ever met. Again, this just added to the Italian-ness of the experience. When the French are rude, they are just rude, but when the Italians are rude, they are fiery and exciting. I collect rude people. My number one rude person was a waiter in Venice. He was so rude that I kept going back to him every day. He would throw the plate of food on the table without looking at where he was putting it; he poured water over my arm; instead of saying, 'Are you ready to order?' he just shouted, 'Speak!' He was amazing. The other staff eventually knew I was coming to the restaurant because I was enjoying him. On the fourth day, when I sat down, he told me to leave. Well, he actually said, 'Geta outa.' It was one of the greatest compliments I have ever received.

He wasn't a patch on our lovely receptionist, however. As we approached the desk, she put out one hand to stop me and, with her other hand open, she sighed with the most Italian accent ever, 'Credit card.' My heart jumped. Here was the woman I'd been looking to add to my collection and she was only in her early thirties. So much potential.

I gave her my credit card and she spoke again with disdain and a hint of hatred. 'Name?'

'O'Shea.'

She looked at me as if I was shit on her shoe and said, 'First name?'

'Oh, Bernard.' Then I hit her early with my Italian: 'Bernardo.'

This just brought her to a new level of hatred. 'Is your name Bernardo Shea or Bernard O'Shea?'

'Eh, it's Bernard O'Shea. I'll spell it for you.'

This was a mistake. 'I know how to spell.' I was transfixed. She was brilliant and after a ten-minute conversation or, as my wife called it, 'a row' over how I spell my own name, we headed up the stairs with our key.

My wife looked at me. 'You're delighted now, aren't you?' And I was.

The next day we both went down to the pool. My wife went ahead of me because I had brought no swimming trunks or suntan lotion. My lovely, angry receptionist – let's call her Angela because that was her name – wasn't on, so I had to ask the new, friendly receptionist where I could buy swimming trunks. She told me I could buy some in the hotel shop, along with suntan lotion. She then asked me, 'Is there anything else I can helpa you with, Mr Ashea?'

Damn, she was ruining my experience. However, my withdrawal symptoms were short-lived. As I entered the tiny little hotel shop, who was there, speaking to the woman behind the counter, only Angela. 'Essscusay,' I said, knowing it would drive her mental.

'Yes?' said the friendly assistant.

'I'm looking for swimming trunks and suntan lotion, please.' She pointed into a tiny little corner of the shop where there were three pairs of red trunks: small, medium and large. The large size barely covered my hand, let alone my distinctive flabby forty-inch waistline. I had, however, no option, so I bought them.

Then I asked her for suntan lotion. 'Sure, whata factuuur?'

I thought for a bit, then said, 'Seventy, please.' There was silence and then Angela burst out laughing – so hard she actually got off the stool she was sitting on. She screamed in hysterics and shouted in my face: 'Seyvontie? There is no seyvontie. What is de eyeist we 'ave, Maria?' Maria, who seemed totally unaffected by Angela's roasting of me, looked at the bottles and said, 'A fifteen is de eyeist. Nobody ever ask for a seyvontie. I don't think it exist.'

Angela had now soared into the lead of the list of my favourite rude people on the planet. To actually mock me in front of another person was taking her to a new level. I took my tiny trunks and suntan lotion and headed down to the pool on a high, with the added confidence of my new ability to swim. It would be the first time I ever swam on a holiday. When I got to the pool, my wife had found a corner in the shade and was reading her book. Instantly I had a problem. The pool was surrounded by beautiful people. Everybody had a perfect BMI and tanned skin. Nobody, and I mean nobody, had brought Tayto or sandwiches or even a large two-litre bottle of Country Spring.

I had actually brought a few cans and quickly hid them under the lounger. Even though I was desperate to get out of the Irish weather, I prayed to the Irish Jesus – not the Italian Jesus (the Italian Jesus, in my mind, doesn't answer prayers unless you're well dressed and have had at least two espressos)

– that another Paddy would arrive on the scene and do a belly flop into the pool. I looked around again and realised that continentals spend their whole lives concentrating on what they look like. It's a massive generalisation but it's true. Has a good-looking Italian man ever told you the story about the time he soiled himself on the Westport train because he drank too much the night before? No. I'm not a proud person. They say pride comes before a fall, but I wouldn't know. If you suffer with self-confidence issues, just get rid of all pride and you will become the most confident person in the world. You will enter into a mental space I like to call the D-GAF Zone or the Don't Give a F##k Zone. So I tore off my Ireland away soccer jersey and revealed my new red hotel swimming trunks. Lake Garda was getting a glimpse of the whitest man the world has ever seen.

I jumped in and swam a full length of the pool. After a few laps, I noticed people looking at me but also trying to avoid looking at me. In a perverse way, I thought maybe, just maybe, they wished they had my beautiful pale Irish features; or maybe they were all thinking, 'Wow, what an amazing swimmer.'

In the corner of my eye I could see Lorna running towards me. She beckoned me to get out of the pool, but I stood my ground. I was quite enjoying my dip. She started to say, in that loud voice, 'Bernard, can you come here?'

I hadn't finished my swim, so I proudly replied, 'I'm swimming, honey.' It was only when I started to do the backstroke that I knew something was wrong, because everybody got out of the pool. I heard Lorna roar, 'Get out of the pool!' I stood up and shouted back 'Why?' And then came the reply no man ever, ever, ever, wants to hear at any time in his life: 'Because everybody can see your balls.'

I looked down. There they were, poking out from my way-too-tight Italian-bought trunks. They looked like two small Jack Russell dogs poking their heads around a corner after smelling a turkey. I tried desperately to put them back in, while I was in the water, but it only made them more prominent. I've learned this: there is no graceful way to exit a swimming pool with your balls sticking out of a pair of shorts that do not fit you. If you put your hands around them, it's even weirder. I did think of doing nothing. Pretend everything was fine, almost in defiance. But it was too late. If you've ever seen a video of a penguin falling from the ice into water, well, that's exactly how I got out of the pool, except in reverse. Lorna had a towel waiting and wrapped my mid-section up, like a chip-pan fire. We scurried back to our rooms blistering red, not from sunburn but embarrassment.

For the rest of the day everybody was quietly noticing us. Lorna kept saying, 'I'm f##king lumped in with you.' It was typical that literally everywhere we went we bumped into people who had attended The Super Balls. Eventually, we found a little café off the beaten track, near a village called Limone. When the waitress came over to us to take our order, she looked at me and asked me, 'You Irish?'

'Yes,' I replied. I was wearing my Ireland football jersey so I thought that was how she'd recognised me, but no.

'Oh,' she said. 'You stay in Garda in 'otel. My sister work there. She say you swim this morning.'

Lorna just got up and said, 'We're leaving.' Literally everybody within a thirty-mile radius knew of the red-haired Irish ball-flasher.

That evening, back at the hotel, Angela was on reception. I tried leaving without her noticing me, but she did. 'Excuse,

Mista Ashea.' She asked me if I could be mindful and wear appropriate swimwear in the pool.

I tried to fight my corner and tell her that it was her fault for selling the trunks, but she told me that lots of people wear them and don't have this issue. I then proceeded to tell her forcefully that it wasn't my fault that my testicles did not fit snugly into the trunks I'd been sold by the hotel.

The next day, we went to the large town of Verona. I bought new trunks. When we got back to the hotel, I put them on and headed down to the pool. 'F##k 'em,' I thought. 'Just because they escaped once that does not make me a pervert.' My wife declined my offer to join me, so I flip-flopped my way brazenly through reception and headed poolside. When I arrived, nobody was in the pool. They were all hanging around the side of it looking at a lanky Italian teenager who was going up and down with a big stupid fishing net in the water. I dived straight in.

They were all shouting and roaring at me: 'No, no, no.' I stood up, looked to make sure the mouse was in the house – it was – then prepared to lay into them. I was sick of their good looks, tanned skin and perfect BMIs. I paid for a hotel with a pool and I was going to swim in it.

'Getta out, Getta out!' the big lanky teenager was roaring at me. It was then that I noticed a large brown log that looked like a poo heading in my direction. In fact, it was a poo. There were lots of poos. A toddler had defecated in the pool and it had dispersed evenly though the water. Everyone was consoling his parents and making sure the kid was okay. I panicked and tried to get out, so quickly that I scraped my leg off the side wall. I was furious. I'd flashed, by accident, a bit of testicle and this family get away with SHITTING in the pool?

Nobody was coming over to me to ask how my leg was or to offer any help, now that I was covered in poo pool water. In fact, quite the opposite. The big lanky teenager started to lecture me about diving into the pool while there were signs up. The 'signs' were as big as Post-it notes. It resulted in me having an argument with him and two German men about my behaviour. I snapped and in my best Irish accent told them to …

That evening, as we were checking out, six days before we were supposed to, my wife asked Angela if she would recommend a hotel that would suit us. She told us about a beautiful little hotel that was in a similar price range, beside a small lakeside town only thirty minutes away by taxi. I was really confused by Angela. She was the most hateful, arrogant Italian I had ever met, yet here she was helping us – well, my wife – out of a smelly, flashy situation.

My wife asked, 'Why this hotel?' Angela looked across at me and said, 'Because it don't have a swimming pool.'

7. He tried to wash lino tiles in the dishwasher and he ruined my new yoga mat.

Lorna and I have always argued over housework. At times it has escalated into full- scale warfare, from 'I've done the hoovering for the last two years' or 'You have never once taken out the bins' to the extreme. For example, I argued in the Great Row of '09, two years into our relationship, that if one of us does the washing-up two days in a row, the other person has to do it for the rest of the week.

I realise I've lost every argument with my wife when she says, 'Yeah, okay, I'll agree to that.' That essentially means that there is a fatal flaw in my argument and that I've lost. In the Great Row of '09, I said something like 'I'm never ever, ever doing the bedsheets and duvets again.' This was, and still is, the job I hate the most. I'd prefer to cut off my own feet with a blunt hacksaw than have an MMA fight with a duvet cover and duvet. Honestly, it is the one thing in life I detest. I've sat for hours on the side of our bed YouTubing 'how to put a duvet into a duvet cover', instead of just doing it. Everybody has their own method. Mine is, I refuse to do it.

As for those 'fitted sheets' that NEVER *ever* stay on the corner of the bed but always pop off the corner of the mattress, and only when I'm about to keel over due to lack of sleep. Then, having surrendered its grip on the grey, spongy corner-of-the-mattress cliff face, the sheet rolls itself into a polyester snake that burns or dislocates my collar bone, if I dare sleep on it. I have daydreams about two men packing a fitted sheet delivery van, laughing to themselves at the torture they are about to inflict on ordinary people.

But the dishes … oh, the dishes. That's a different kettle of unwashed colanders altogether.

First, let me describe the Great Row of '09. There were no winners that year, just a rota. My wife is obsessed with three things: lists, lampshades and rotas. She has constantly argued for the implementation of a rota for jobs around the house, or, as our American friends would say, 'chores'. I have no problem with that, because I think I do more housework.

The original row began when I suggested my wife do a simple task – the dishes. A stand-off ensued and two weeks later, the Leaning Tower of Pisa had been replicated on the side of the sink, held together with bitterness and baked-bean cement. I felt I had washed the dishes all week. She felt she had. I felt that if I did them again, I'd become 'the person who does the dishes' in our relationship. My friend Neil told me that, when he was younger, his mother used to make him do the hoovering all the time. When he protested, his brothers said, 'But you're good at the hoovering.' That's what happens. One day you're doing your 'turn', the next you're doing the dishes every day because you're 'good at them'. This wasn't happening to me.

Now, you are most definitely asking yourself, 'Why don't they have a dishwasher?' Well, we didn't, because prior to my wife and me meeting, she chose to put a tumble dryer in the available space under the sink in her flat. She also stuck rigidly to her principles: 'There's only two of us, we don't need one.' Well, on 30 March 2009, we needed one, because neither of us wanted to wash 22 plates.

It became the most bizarre argument I've ever had with anybody, ever. When we were watching the telly (we could back then, we had no kids) we would talk about work and plans, the usual ether of life. When we were in the bedroom, it was very amicable too (we could back then, we had no kids). In fact, we would go out, have drinks, pop to the cinema – it was good. We were, dare I say it, a 'normal couple'. But when we were within touching distance of the sink and the unwashed ceramic tower of stubbornness, it got bad … really bad. There were tears, pointing at it with ruined mascara around the eyes: 'Look at it, all stacked up, smelly and rotten because you have to be right all the time.' To which she would reply, 'Stop crying, ya big wimp, just clean them.' (I regularly left my make-up on after a TV gig because I'm obsessed with looking younger.)

I let rip my *Braveheart* line: 'I don't understand. Why can't we just get a dishwasher?'

This time she seemed invested in my plea. We sat down to hammer out a deal. She would agree to getting a dishwasher if I did the dishes now.

'Hold on, so we can get one tomorrow?'

'Yes,' she replied.

I had to think about it. It is very rare that my wife will agree with me, especially during a row. There's a catch, I thought, there has to be a catch. So I suggested what we should have agreed upon from the very start. 'Let's do them together?'

'No. If you want your dishwasher, you do them,' she muttered, with a strong emphasis on '*your*'.

'*My* dishwasher?'

'Well, I'm okay without one. I always do my turn. It's you who has the problem.'

I lost it. 'Leave them there. I'm not touching them, ever, and when your friends call around, they'll see the mess.'

Now this was a really mean thing to say, but it's true in every relationship. When your partner cleans the house to a really high standard, it's generally because a friend or relative is calling over. Back then, we had no kids, so the clean-up would have been minimal. Now, when our friends visit our house, the second they leave, a bomb full of toys, Lego and milk mould explodes from the utility room, where we pushed all the mess seconds before our visitors arrived at the hall door. When we have visitors around these days, we live in fear of them opening the door under the stairs, because they could die from the blast of coats, Paw Patrol playpens and number seven-size nappies that is held in there by a combination of pressure and extreme shame. (For those of you who don't know, *Paw Patrol* is an animated show featuring rescue dogs as heroes.) I did try to install one of those cool storage drawers there recently, but that's another story (see no. 28).

But, getting back to the dishes, the following is a timeline of events leading up to the apex of The Great Row of '09:

30 March 2009

15:40: Lorna has left the house. Good – I'm hungry. Bad – I've nothing to eat off or with.

15:41: I leave the house and get the bus into town.

16:45: Nearly an hour later I'm in a popular kebab shop in Dublin's Temple Bar. I order the chicken shish kebab.

17:20: It's raining, so I decide to walk home because I'm a f##king eejit.

17:35: I'm walking past the bakery on James's Street. I pop in for a sneaky bun. I normally get two: one for me and one for Lorna. I'm in fight mode, though, so I only get two: one for me and one for me.

17:38: I'm walking past St James's Gate, the Guinness Brewery, close to our flat, when a very wet and a very familiar blue Toyota Corolla stops at the lights. It's Lorna.

17:38:40: I go to get into the car. The door is locked. I'm looking into the car. Lorna is staring straight ahead, ignoring me. Lights turn green. Car moves off.

17:48: I arrive home. Wet. Ready to tackle my wife for not giving me a lift home. She has brought it to a whole new level.

17:49: Having prepared a meal of potato waffles and scrambled egg, my wife is eating it off PAPER PLATES.

17:51: The conversation goes like this:

Me: Paper plates? That's how far this has gone? Fine, sure I can eat off paper plates too.

Lorna: Get your own.

Me: Why? Have you hidden them, like you hid the giant Milka hazelnut bar you brought back from holidays? Well, guess what, it's between your hot water bottle and the linen sheets under the bed – and I've eaten some of it.

I had gone too far. The fact that I found my wife's chocolate stash and had gone poking around on her side of the bed in the first place was … okay, I was wrong.

She also hates it when I walk on her yoga mat and makes me clean it. It drives me bonkers. 'Your shoes could have been anywhere,' she says.

'Well, stop leaving it on the ground, then.' If there is a fourth thing she's obsessed with it's buying yoga mats. But paper plates? That was a new level. A new level that I couldn't stoop to. Where would I go from here?

Eureka! While she watched TV, I ran the hot water into the sink. I squirted washing-up liquid in. I could see her trying not to look to see what was happening. Was I caving? Was I going to do the dishes?

'OK,' I said. 'Have it your way.' I washed one plate and one set of cutlery. Put them in the empty press and left.

Well, I didn't exactly leave, I went to the petrol station to get a Twix. Wait …

18:15:	I go to the nearby petrol station to get a Twix.
18:22:	Both of us are sitting in front of the telly.
18:23:	I have a genius idea.
18:25:	I go to the press. Get out my clean plate and cutlery. I proceed to eat my Twix on a clean plate with my clean knife and fork. Paper plates, *touché*.
18:26:	My wife leaves the room.
18:26:	Shite. Should have done the dishes.
18:27:	Front door slams.
18:27:	Shite, should *really* have done the dishes.
18:28:	I finish the Twix.
18:29:	I start to wash the dishes.
18:40:	Dishes are clean.
22:40:	Having decided to let them air dry, I put the dishes away.
23:10:	My wife returns home.
	I said sorry, expecting the reply to be 'You always say sorry.' It wasn't. We decided to get a dishwasher. I ordered it online. It's going to be delivered Wednesday. That simple.

01:12:   Lying in bed I realise *no, not that simple*. I did the dishes and I'll have to wait around between 9 a.m. and the year 2057 and *I'm* the one who is wrong? No way.

01:13:   I fall asleep.

Wednesday 1 April

Completely forgetting it was April Fools' Day, I waited patiently for the delivery of our new dishwasher. I felt extremely proud of myself, having moved the tumble dryer into the box room all by myself. This time I didn't dislocate my kneecap as I had done the last time I moved something, nor did I have to call 'a man' to help me. The gap under the sink looked strange. It constantly amazes me the dirt that can build up under appliances. A little bit of me hoped we would never clean the dishes, because I'm obsessed with the story of Alexander Fleming, leaving his dishes for a month and discovering a mould on them which became penicillin. It was only years later that a friend of mine explained, 'Petri dishes, ya f##king eejit.' Anyhow, I didn't discover any Nobel prize-winning antibiotics: instead I opted for cleaning the floor where the dryer had been.

I thought a cloth and water would do the job. Thirty minutes later, it hadn't. I then tried bleach, but the dirt was so ingrained by the heat of the dryer, it was impossible to remove. I should have just left it, but I had a brainwave. My plan was to pull up the tiles and put them in the dishwasher when it arrived. Sounds simple, and it was, but there was a flaw, a fundamental flaw in my logic.

Four hours, and five tiles removed with a large nail file, later, the buzzer rang.

'Delivery for O'Shea.'

'Yeah that's me. I'll pop down.'

I helped him to put the dishwasher in the lift and when we arrived at my apartment, he wheeled it into the kitchen.

'What's wrong with the floor?' he said.

'Oh, I took up the tiles.'

'Why?'

'Because they were dirty.'

He looked me directly in the eye. 'But you could have cleaned them.'

'I tried, but there was a dryer there for years and it baked the dirt onto them.'

He inhaled with gusto and tiredness. 'Well, I can't put a dishwasher on them boards. It needs tiles, or even lino.'

Thinking quickly, I came to the horrible realisation: 'I have no lino.' And that I'd possibly made a hames – again – of the simplest household task.

There was silence. Then the man said, 'Look, you can put new tiles down and I'll show you how to install the dishwasher. It's easy.'

Straightaway I could hear my wife's voice: 'No, no, no, no, no, you are not going near the plumbing.' But the man showed me, no, reassured me, that I could do it. 'Look, just connect that grey pipe to that outlet, turn the red tap to the right all the way, and that's it. Otherwise, I can take it back, but you mightn't get it until next week. I'm flat out.'

He left. I wept.

Two hours, three espressos and four YouTube videos later, I decided that laying floor tiles was not going to be a possibility. But I had an idea! My wife loves yoga. She had recently bought a new yoga mat, which she loved. Yoga mats are like lino, right? I couldn't find her old one ... but I did find her new one. I thought I could put the dishwasher on the yoga mat, connect it up and rush into town to buy a new mat to replace the one I'd used and no one would know.

I put the dishwasher on the yoga mat, connected it and turned it on for the 30-minute cycle to check that it was working. It was! I stood back and blushed with pride. I felt the testosterone pulse through my body, as if I was a lion in a Formula One car shooting an Old Spice commercial. I was so proud of me. But I had no time for self-pride; I had to get into town to replace the yoga mat before Lorna got home. I threw the dishes and floor tiles from the last two days into the new dishwasher and selected 'eco wash'. The little digital display said 3:30. Perfect. I had no dishwasher tablets, but being the amazing improviser I am, I just squirted washing-up liquid into the machine, because it's the same thing. (It isn't.) I grabbed my keys and coat and bolted into town to get the yoga mat.

I'm always intimidated by any shop that has displays of products that you know you can't touch. I'm sure somebody had gone to great effort to arrange the yoga mats in a tepee formation in the shop, but the colour and brand of the one I'd used for temporary lino was right in the middle. I had no time. I desperately wanted to pull it out and when the tepee fell apart, say, 'Oh, I'm so sorry, I didn't think that would happen.'

I was going to, until a very skinny man wearing a wool hat and a pair of pyjamas stopped me. 'I'll see if we have one in the back.' I've never worked in a shop, but I imagine 'the back' to be a magical kingdom full of tranquil overflowing stacks of products handed to shop assistants by mermaids. It's also apparently where staff go for a break and a smoke. My man must have gone to India to check because he took FOR EVER. In hindsight, it was probably only two minutes max, but Christ, I was running out of time.

'Sorry, we have none in stock,' he said when he returned.

'That's okay. I'll take the display one.'

He paused. Why was he pausing? Sell me the stupid mat, I thought.

'I'll just have to make a quick call to see if I can do that,' he said with real seriousness.

I swear to God, I thought I was going to be the first person in the world to kill another human being in a yoga shop. I wanted to tell him everything: the row over the dishes. Me ordering the dishwasher. My decision to pull up the tiles. Using my wife's yoga mat as temporary lino. The delivery man who'd looked at me like I was a failure and my eventual triumph at installing a dishwasher.

He was on the phone for ages. He eventually hung up and approached me.

'The mat – is it for yoga or Pilates use?'

'It's for yoga.'

'And is it for yourself?'

Now, for some reason, I hadn't killed him by now. I just needed that mat, so instead of telling him that it was for my wife, I said, 'Yeah, it's for me.'

'Oh, okay … and what weight are you?'

Was this guy serious? He was asking me my weight? Just sell me the mat, I thought. I could feel my blood pressure rising. I had an hour max before Lorna came home and today would, of course, be the day she decided to yoga. If that is the verb for doing yoga.

I had to ask. 'What difference does it make what weight I am?'

'I don't think this mat could hold your weight.'

There was at least a good thirty-second pause before he started roaring laughing. 'Ah, I'm only joking … April Fool.'

He tried to wash lino tiles in the dishwasher and he ruined my new yoga mat.

I wanted to f##king kill him. I could see the Pathé Newsreel-style headlines flutter in my mind: Man Kills Yoga Salesman in Downward Dog Massacre. April Fool's Day Yogatrocity. Yoga Fury Strikes a Killer Pose. I grabbed the mat. Twenty minutes later I was running in the rain with a yoga mat under my arm, desperately trying to get home before my wife. I ran the mile and a half from the city centre to our front door in twenty-three minutes. Yes, I was in a hurry, but I also wanted to put the cardio into my calorie counter (I'm obsessed with losing weight) and twenty minutes of cardio in my mind meant that I could eat a spoon of Nutella from the jar.

I made it home before her. I turned the key in the door, full of pride, and walked into the biggest f##king-eejit mistake of my life.

The flat was full of bubbles. Yes, bubbles. Apparently, you're not supposed to put washing-up liquid in a dishwasher. I stood at the door for at least ten minutes. When I did walk through the mountain of bubbles, I couldn't breathe. I eventually made my way to the kitchen window, which I opened, and frantically started to push the giant blocks of bubbles out into the clear blue Dublin sky. It took me fifteen minutes to get rid of most of them, but I was left with a problem. The flat was drenched. There was soapy water everywhere.

I got the biggest towel I could find and started to dry every surface. It was nearly half-five. I was exhausted.

My wife arrived home and before I could open my mouth, she said, 'You're not going to believe it, but the laneway is covered in clouds of bubbles.'

'What? That's mad. What do they look like?'

'Just … giant bubble clouds … did you get a yoga mat?'

I could have, should have, lied. But reluctantly I told the truth. A barrage of whys flews in my direction, followed by an

AK-47 assault on my intelligence. It only stopped when she looked around. 'Oh, my God, the place is immaculate.'

You see? Method in my madness.

8. He's a hypochondriac. A simple cold for everyone else becomes triple pneumonia for him.

My wife proudly tells anybody who will listen that I'm a hypochondriac. She thinks it's hilarious. However, what she doesn't know is that my hypochondria is just part of the constant battle of who is sicker, her or me. It's a bit like the first holiday you take together: the first time your partner gets sick, you are like Florence Nightingale, hovering over them, damp facecloth in hand. By the time you've been together more than a year, and particularly if you have children, they could have malaria and you'd think, so what? It could be worse – and the dishwasher needs emptying.

Lorna thinks it's hilarious that I tell people I got pneumonia last year. She says that no doctor ever told me that. True, but when I took our daughter Olivia to the doctor, I had a chest infection and the doctor asked me how long I'd had it. I told her half a year, and she told me to get an X-ray of my lungs. Now, being a good hypochondriac, I didn't go for an X-ray, as it happens, but the doctor had insisted on checking me because I was so unwell. See, Lorna, the doctor checked *me* and if you have a chest infection for months and need an X-ray, I'm pretty sure that's called pneumonia, so ha!

I've also dislocated my knee cap twice – fact. I don't just *think* I've dislocated it; I've actually seen it leave my leg twice and so has Lorna. The first time I dislocated it was playing football and the second time was when we first went to my mother's with Olivia. I was playing with my niece, running after her, and 'pop'. Lorna saw it and still she thinks I'm a hypochondriac?

I get sick because I get whatever the kids get. I was a healthy human being up until the age of thirty, then whatever my kids would bring home, they would infect me with. The minute one of them sneeze, that's it, I get it. I'm like an infant illness-absorbing sponge.

I'm not a hypochondriac, because my doctor said I couldn't be. Why? Well, the last time I visited him and told him that my wife thinks I'm a hypochondriac, he said, 'Well you've only visited me twice in six years. You're one of those good hypochondriacs who don't bother their doctors.' You see, Lorna, our GP doesn't think I'm one. He also has a mug with *Please do not confuse your Google search with my medical degree* written on it. This, however, I am guilty of.

I've a bit of a penchant for reading medical journals online and also googling everything that ails me. It is one of the online fetishes that infuriates my wife the most. '*Go to the doctor!*' she screamed at me when I told her I thought I'd had a brain haemorrhage. It turned out that my back tooth was pushing a muscle in the back of my eye and that's where the pain was coming from. But then our doctor told me he was going to take my bloods. This filled me with fear. I'm a trypanophobic. I'm terrified of dinosaurs. No, just kidding: I have an overwhelming fear of needles, especially hypodermic needles, so much so that I can't even look at them on the telly or hear anyone talk about them.

On one of our holidays in Greece, when we still took holidays in Greece as a couple, I contracted salmonella. It got bad – really bad. Lorna cared for me for five days in a warm hotel room on a small Greek island. I knew she loved me when she had to change the towel I was lying on every two hours. Nothing says 'love' more than 'Okay, shift over, I need to change your shitty towel.' Eventually, when I started to hallucinate, she brought me to the local hospital. It was then that she found out my deepest, darkest fear. The doctor told me he would have to give me an injection and then put me on an intravenous drip to rehydrate me. In an answer that I am constantly slagged about, I replied, 'Is it totally necessary?'

My wife who, let me remind you, changed my shitty towels for five days, burst out laughing. The kind Greek doctor looked at me, completely confused, before saying, 'Yes, it is necessary.'

'I have a fear of needles.' There, I thought, I've said it, it's out.

'That's okay.' He shouted 'Vera!' and his assistant calmly sailed into the room. She was a big woman with the darkest eyes and she was wearing Superman slippers. The doctor said something in Greek and Vera looked at me. Then Vera responded in Greek, looking in my direction, and the doctor said very firmly, 'nay nay', which always confuses me because I think it means 'yes'. She left the room and, a minute later, she returned with a box of kids' toys. I was so dehydrated and out of my mind, I thought I was going to be forced to play some sick and twisted game with Vera for the doctor. Then the doctor brought the box over and said, 'Which one would you pick?' I hesitated, but eventually picked out the Fisher-Price phone. I was just about to tell him my theory about how Fisher-Price get most technological advances backwards – i.e. car phone/phone car – when I felt a strong pinch in my arm. He had just gone and given me a prod without me noticing.

He then said, 'You have Slinky in Ireland?' He took a big spring out of the box and then asked my wife the same question. He then started to tell me that when he was young, a cousin of his mother in America would send over a small box of used toys every year for his birthday along with some biscuits. I was desperate to tell him that's how USA assorted biscuits in Ireland came about, but before I could, Vera Greeked out, 'Peppermint Mentos', which I learned from the waiters in the restaurants we visited means 'finished'. But finished what? Vera had just gone and put the drip into me without me noticing. Those crafty Greeks. I only spent six days there and most of it on the toilet, but what nice people.

Fast forward five years. I'm in my doctor's surgery in Dublin. I tell him my fear. He reaches under his desk and guess what? Yep, a box of toys. There I am, a man in his thirties making a pretend phone call to his fears on a Fisher-Price phone while a trained medical professional, who deals with really sick people, takes a few vials of blood.

It transpired that I was vitamin B12-deficient. It's very common in Irish people. I had to buy B12 vitamins and would leave them in the wine rack over the fridge. As the space in the wine rack (which is never used for wine) is as hotly contested in our house as apartment space in downtown Manhattan, they always get moved.

One morning, as a joke, I shouted up the stairs to Lorna, 'Where are my meds?'

Lorna proceeded to tell me that vitamins are not 'meds'. I called them my meds anyway, just to piss her off. Yeah, she changed my Greek poopy towels but I like to call them 'my meds' anyway.

* * *

Since we've had children, I've noticed a new game creep into our lives – an almost subconscious game of chess that we play around our ailments, called 'Who is sicker?' I'm thinking of turning it into a new game show for TV, based directly on what happens in our house. I get the man flu, and for some unknown reason Lorna gets a pain in her stomach. I start talking about my bad left knee (the one I've dislocated – *twice*) and she starts talking about her bad shoulder. What I really find funny (some people find this not so funny) is the complete lack of sympathy that we have developed for each other over time. When I think of my salmonella poisoning in Greece and how amazingly Lorna looked after me and how she now bemoans my constant ailments, I can't help thinking that I've become the equivalent of an old telly.

When we grew up in rural Ireland in the 1980s, all we had on our TV were the two national stations, RTÉ 1 and 2. That telly brought us literally everything we knew: football matches, fashions, news and the odd salacious film put on very late at night. Even though we loved that telly, because it was an old Hitachi, it began to gradually break. Unlike the flat screens of today, it was a big old cathode tube-thumper and when it wasn't working, we would just walk up to it and hit it on its side. That TV took some punishment, but we needed it in our lives and I certainly loved it.

That's the way I see my wife's love for me changing over time. Does she care when I get one of my hypochondriac episodes? Or even real flu? Or when I dislocate my knee cap … again? Possibly not as much as she used to, but she still loves me enough to get up and give me a good old thump and hope I work again. I am my wife's old, sick TV that still does the job. I just hope she never wants to trade me in for a flat screen.

9. He wore a brown cardigan to our first date.

There are lots of advantages to being married, but the biggest has to be avoiding Tinder dating and, if I'm brutally honest, not always having to look great or, in my case, even good for your better half. I once said to my wife, 'If you ever leave me, please set me up with somebody before you slam the door and go.' Her reply? 'I won't be slamming any door; it will be you who'll be leaving.'

Tinder and online dating seem way too vicious and scary for me. I dread to think of anybody swiping negatively on my face, in an online or offline world. Besides, I was dreadful at chatting up women. It was only because a friend was beside me the night I met Lorna that I asked her out at all. He said, 'You should get her number. She likes you.' Thank God he was there because I could never read the signs, positive or negative. I don't even know what 'the signs' are. There are thousands of YouTube videos dedicated to reading these elusive non-verbal smoke signals and how to respond. It frightens me. I had one go-to chat up line … 'Hello'. If that didn't work, I was gone. Now there seem to be complicated strategies of timelines and tan-lines, just to meet somebody. I'm a sitting duck. Lorna, please don't leave. If you want an affair, just don't give out to me about him, okay? I'm a stayer.

Little did I know, though, that my thoughtful wife nearly didn't go on a second date with me because of my favourite brown wool reversible jacket, or, as she called it, 'a cardigan'.

On our first date, she was late. I didn't mind. I'm always on time when I'm on a date, or if there is food involved. So we met and went for a drink and, later, some Chinese food. I thought it went really well, until, years later, she told me, 'When you showed up in a big brown cardigan, I thought, "Oh, Jesus, I have to walk around with him wearing that yoke." I wanted to stay inside, because I was mortified to be seen with you wearing it around. The second night I met you, I hid across the road to see if you were going to be wearing it again. Luckily for you, you weren't. You didn't lose it, either. I threw it into a recycling bin in the shopping centre.'

I was shocked. I thought that clothes didn't matter to my wife at all. Then, recently, I've heard her say things like 'Oh, a man in a suit … yes, please.' What? I never wear suits. In fact, I don't own a suit. I come from a practical foundation when it comes to clothes. All items have to have the following:

Pockets: I can never understand why women's clothes, especially dresses, don't have pockets. Where do people who wear dresses keep their stuff? And I hate holding bags. I know it's petty and ungentlemanly, but it's a big pain in the hole holding a sparkly gold clutch bag for an entire night.

Warmth: There are times when I look at guys wearing T-shirts and jeans in the middle of December and think, yes, you fit very well into that Abercrombie T-shirt, but regardless of your muscle mass and how many gains you've made, you're going to catch a cold.

Waterproofing: I live in Ireland. The literal translation of 'Ireland' is 'Land where it rains all the time'. Well, it isn't, but it should be. I look at most clothes in shop windows in Ireland and automatically think, 'That will get destroyed in the rain.'

Finally, they have to have built-in flexibility and comfort. This is a problem I've had with clothes since my twenties. My weight goes up and down all the time. It fluctuates so rapidly that even typing the word 'fluctuates' gives it enough time to go up again. This poses a problem. Either you end up buying clothes all the time, or, like me, just keep wearing whatever fits you until it becomes threadbare. I hate those people who can eat anything they want and never put on weight, mostly because they always know their size and never have to try things on in shops. My wife, over the years, has tried to convince me that you shouldn't try things on just to see if they fit, but also to see if they suit you. My thinking, however, is if clothes fit me, they suit me.

My main issue with trying clothes on in shops stems from childhood experiences. I grew up with three older sisters. I was the youngest. You should have seen the hand-me-downs. I nearly had to do my first job interview in my sister's trouser suit. I would always want to go shopping with them because we only had two TV stations and the dog consistently burst my ball or died, but when it came to my turn to try on clothes, I would always want to try them on in the changing rooms. But my mother would always come out with the statement that haunted my early shopping expeditions: 'No, you can try them on here,' indicating the shop floor, followed by 'Sure who'll be looking at you?'

'EVERYBODY, MAMMY' is what I wanted to scream. So, there I would be, shadily trying on a pair of trousers, or 'slacks' as my parents called them, between the rows of clothes on the shop floor. I would peer up above the mammy coat rack and see hundreds of other boys trying on their clothes on the shop floor too.

It is a sad day in every mother's life when a child, particularly her son, doesn't want her to pick out his clothes. My mother constantly tells the story of when I was going to secondary school and getting a new coat. I told her to put it in the bag and then walk out of the shop without me. Teenage boys can be cruel, but it's our hormones and OUR REALLY EMBARRASSING PARENTS that are the cause of it. Let's just say, some adolescent hormones still remain in my bloodstream. That teenage banishment will never happen to me, of course, as my children are going to remain cute little loving toddlers who think I'm amazing for ever. My mother and sisters disagree.

Luckily for me, my wife only likes shopping on her own, or, to put it in her words: 'I hate shopping with you.' I don't mind. I just hate browsing. What's the point in aimlessly wandering around shops 'just looking'? I like to know exactly what I want and just go and buy it. Trying things on is a major roadblock in the fluidity of my plan.

* * *

The one time we did go shopping together resulted in one of the most mortifying experiences of my life. Before we had children only God knows what we did with our spare time. Sometimes I think the government is using us as an experiment, probing us and the little sleep we get to try and find the elusive answer to 'What do people do with all that spare time before the kids come along?' One Saturday BK (Before Kids) we decided to go to a shopping centre about thirty miles outside Dublin. Americans and Continentals find this hilarious. They would easily pop in their car and drive thirty miles to get milk, never mind designer socks. In Ireland thirty miles is still classified as a journey, where people still text each other to tell them where they're going, in the event of a nuclear catastrophe. Regardless of how modern we have become as a nation, a lot of us still feel the need to bring sandwiches on a journey that could last longer than half an hour.

When we arrived, we had our usual row about where to park. Lorna wanted to park inside the shop that she wanted to visit, whereas I wanted to park in space, i.e. as far away from other cars as possible. Eventually, we were walking toward the outlet and the strangest thing happened: for the first time and last since we met, my wife took my hand and led me to the shop she wanted ME to shop in. 'This shop does really nice stuff,' she said with an air of authority. It was one of those clothes shops where I can never make out the difference between the men's and women's sections. It was also one of those stores where the staff look at you as if you are a badly designed shite on a half-eaten slipper. The second I walked into the store I could see the young guys behind the counter judging me with their millennial eyes. They knew and I knew that nothing they had would fit me.

Millennials get a hard time, mainly because they are in the wilderness between adolescence and adulthood. I got a hard time as a teenager, too, because I annoyed other people, due to my inbuilt capacity to make everything difficult. But I wasn't called a millennial. I begrudge them for having a group title.

I'm supposedly nearing my MAMIL stage (middle-aged men in Lycra). Thus, our two worlds collided in a shop that was way too trendy for me and my sensible haircut and even more sensible attitude of avoiding paying more than twenty euros for a T-shirt.

Lorna handed me a pair of jeans. Well, she called them jeans; I thought they were tights, or the surgical stockings you're given if you dislocate your knee cap.

'Try them on.'

There was no way I was going to try on skinny jeans. I swear, I actually couldn't get my arm through them.

'They stretch, Bernard,' she said. 'Don't be such an old man – go and try them on.' They were a 32-inch waist. I'm a 34 at my very best. I was a 40-inch waist the day I got married. In fairness, Lorna didn't marry me for my body, so I compromised. I walked up to the counter and asked a girl if they had them in a 34. She said, 'I'll have to check the stock room.' Ah, the magical stock room again, this one where they go to probably judge the big ugly fat culchies in their trendy store.

In fairness, she came back swiftly and said, 'Thirty-two is the largest size this brand does.'

What? I haven't had a 32-inch waist since I was 12 years of age.

I knew the jeans wouldn't fit me, but I was f##ked if I was going to let some 'brand' tell me I couldn't wear their clothes. So off I pounded, all 34-inch waist of me, towards their dressing rooms, or, should I say, barrels. This is another thing about 'trendy, cool' shops. For God's sake, will you just build dressing rooms? Why do they have to be burnt-out cars, old aeroplane toilets or, in this case, a barrel? I felt like saying, 'Excuse me, is the barrel 34 inches in diameter? Because otherwise I can't fit into it.' And why, oh why, do they do the 'saw the person in half' trick with the half-doors? Just put up a full door: nobody wants to see my head and lower legs.

I took off my jeans and started to put on the skinny ones. To my surprise, they did stretch. Until I got to the top of my reproductive system. They just wouldn't budge over the budgie. I should have just calmly taken them off, but oh no. I did the jump-and-pull thing to try and breach my midriff. It didn't work and it resulted in me ripping the lower part of my groin and tearing the zip completely away from the jeans. Oh, the pain. Oh, the pain. Did I mention the pain? I had scarred the welding in my scrotum and couldn't scream, because if I screamed semi-naked, with a zip in my hand, in a barrel, in a shop that was clearly designed for malnourished rock band members, that was also full of millennials, I'd be writing this from a corrections facility now.

I calmed down enough to notice that the price tag was attached to the zip. They were on sale for €280. That was the *sale price*? I could book a flight to Amsterdam and get somebody to do the same thing to me in a barrel, while also visiting a few museums. Even though I was in horrific pain and the shame was also setting in, there was no way this degrading life experience was going to cost me €280. Where was my wife? She made me do this.

I had to do that casual and cool call from my barrel, 'Lorna', in a way that sounded like everything was under control. No response.

Then the girl from behind the counter walked over. 'Everything okay?'

'Yeah, fine,' I said, but both of us knew there was something wrong, as I'd been in the barrel now for a good ten minutes.

'There's a mirror out here if you want to see them on.'

I had to think quickly. Why hadn't I left the barrel yet? I had the perfect response: 'Eh, no, I'm grand, thanks.' What is it with Irish people and the word grand? We say it even if things are horrific. A woman stood up one night at a comedy gig I was performing at and made her way along the row of seats in the audience. I could see she was moving very awkwardly, so I asked her from the stage if she was okay. Her reply? 'I'm grand.' Months later, after another gig, a man approached me and told me that the woman that night was his partner – she'd given birth prematurely that night and she didn't want to make a fuss as she tried to get out of the club. What's more, when her friends rang her in the ambulance, she told them she was 'grand'. In the film *Spartacus,* the famous scene where they all begin to stand up and declare, 'I'm Spartacus,' if you look very closely, there's one Irishman standing up, saying, 'I'm grand,' and sitting down again. The *modus operandi* of Irish people in public is not to make a 'holy show' of themselves. After that, whether or not they get what they set out for doesn't matter.

In my predicament, my reproductive system was being ripped apart, but I didn't care. I just needed to get out of the situation without making a holy show of myself. I grabbed my phone and rang Lorna. She answered, 'WHAT?' The response of true love.

I whispered, 'I'm after hurting myself and ripping the jeans. Come down.' I hung up because I couldn't go into a further lengthy explanation on my scrotomatic issues. There was a queue now for the barrel. The queue's demographic was skinny and impatient. Eventually, Lorna showed up. I ushered her over. 'Get in.'

She joined me in the barrel. 'How the f##k did you do this?'

Then the shop assistant shouted, 'Eh, sorry but the changing rooms are for one person only.' I thrust the zip-less jeans into Lorna's hands. 'Put them back on the rail … please, for me.' She had no option. She scampered over and put them back onto the rail. Niftily, she put the zip into the pocket. I put my jeans back on and shot myself out of the barrel. I made it outside the door of the shop and started 'Go go go'.

Lorna stopped me. '"Go go go"? Are you serious? You ripped your penis on a pair of skinny jeans – you didn't rob a bank. I'm going to look around for another half hour. I'll see you back in the car.'

I was in pain. Not emotionally, but physically. Walking was difficult. I knew I wasn't a skinny jeans guy. Why couldn't I just have said, 'No, I'm not grand'? Who was I kidding? I once read in a medical journal that when women look in a mirror, they always see something wrong, but when a man looks into one, nearly ninety per cent of the time he thinks he's a tiger – a sexy, sexy tiger. The thinking is that testosterone is such a powerful hormone, it can give a man incredible amounts of confidence, or in my case, the arrogance to imagine that I could fit into skinny jeans.

However, we'd made the journey and I needed jeans. I walked into the non-cool jeans shop, strode confidently up to the counter and said, 'I would like a pair of dark blue 501s please: thirty-four-inch waist, thirty-four-inch leg,' knowing most definitely that I wasn't going to try them on. I mightn't be a fashionable man, but thankfully my reproductive system was still intact. I hobbled back to the car, turned to my wife, looked into her eyes and said one of the most romantic things you can say to a woman in the car park of an outlet centre: 'You'll have to drive. I can't do the clutch – it's too painful.'

10. His weapon of choice against a home intruder was a Bag for Life ... and no underwear.

It's impossible to know when you become a man. Is it when you have sex for the first time? Is it when you parallel park for the first time? These two activities could be combined, of course, but it's impossible to know. I grew up with three older sisters and they just seemed to become adult females overnight. I'm still working on my manhood, like a younger sibling trying to grow into a school uniform.

I've always wondered about young men going to war. If I was told I had to be drafted into the army, I'd just tell them, 'I'm not good at fighting,' and hopefully they'd take one look and say 'Okay'. I've never been good at physical conflict: I'm terrified of it. In most romantic films, there's always one brave guy who defends his girlfriend against some brute. I'm not one of those guys. I'd turn to that woman and say, 'Let's leave. I'm terrified.' It wouldn't make for a great scene, but I'd still have my teeth.

I constantly wonder what I'd be like if somebody broke into our house. How would I react? I've always thought that

I'd be stoic and that I'd instinctively do the right thing, but nothing strikes the fear of God into your veins as when you're woken up in the middle of the night by a pregnant woman and told, 'There's somebody in the house.'

During my wife's first pregnancy, I was on tenterhooks. Every groan or move she made, I panicked. 'Is this it? Will I get the bags?' She became so pissed off with me, she told me that if I asked her 'Is this it?' once more, she wouldn't let me in to the birth.

However, I really thought it was happening the night she woke me up in *a hysterical state.* 'Bernard, Bernard, wake up.'

I couldn't help myself. 'Is this it?'

'No, you f##king eejit. There's somebody in the house.'

We lay still, listening. I could hear a weird drilling noise. It was coming from the kitchen.

'They have a drill,' Lorna said.

'Why would they have a drill?' I replied. We began to argue about power-drill semantics, until she said the phrase that pays: 'Are you going to do something about it?'

I always hate it when my wife says that. 'The dishwasher is broken ... Are you going to do something about it?' 'The Wi-Fi isn't working ... Are you going to do something about it?' It's painful enough to hear it when something is broken, but it has the added bonus of becoming physically painful when there might be an intruder in your house.

Of course, my reply was 'What do you want me to do about it?' Her look left me with only one option: become a man and defend our flat, while wearing an AC/DC T-shirt, no underwear and holding my weapon of choice in my hand: a Bag for Life wrapped up tightly to form a deadly, environmentally friendly baton.

I crept quietly into the kitchen and used a lethal form of attack. I shouted 'HELLO' several times, really loudly. As we all know, nothing scares burglars off more than a pale, overweight, semi-naked Irishman shouting, 'HELLO'. I turned on the kitchen light and there it was … nothing. There was no one in the kitchen. However, the weird drilling noise was still coming from the small alcove that connected the kitchen to the bedroom, where there was a narrow window to let in air. I opened the window and could see nothing until I looked down. There were two cats having sex on the ledge. The noise cats make while in congress is horrendous. It's a cross between childbirth and chalk being scraped down a blackboard.

The tomcat looked up at me, as if to say, 'What's the problem, pervert?'

I went into the bedroom and told Lorna. 'Well, what are you going to do about it?'

'Nothing.' Why would I ruin a perfectly nice night of romance?

I got back into bed, but it started again. It got so loud that the window started to vibrate. I got up again and got a sweeping brush, leaning out of the narrow opening and shoving it out. As the top of the brush got to the randy couple, the tomcat started to fight back. He was making love and throwing jabs at the brush at the same time. This guy was impressive. I got the brush right in between them and was trying to shove them off the ledge. It's not a nice sensation, feeling cat-love vibrations through a wooden stick. He was so strong that his claws started to dig into the concrete ledge and I noticed he was still 'going'. Eventually I pushed them off and when they hit the ground, which was only a storey below, they scattered in opposite directions.

I went back to bed, remembering all those nights in college when you think you're about to get off with some girl you fancy, only to have her friend come in and 'brush' you away. Five minutes later: 'ORAGHHHHHH, ORAGHHHHHH, ORAGHHHHH'. The cat was back. This time, when I looked out the window, he was with ANOTHER LADY. I went into the kitchen, filled up a pint glass of water and poured it down on him and his new belle, but he loved it – it almost made the experience better for him.

I could hear Lorna from the bedroom. 'Bernard, do something about it, now.' What was I supposed to do? There was a cat, who was basically on Tinder, using a concrete alcove for fornication: this wasn't 'the Hoover's broken again'. I dragged a wireless speaker across to the windowsill and played loud music against the glass. The cats loved it and almost started to make love in time to 'Around the World'. My thinking had been logical: if I made the glass vibrate, it would throw him off his game. It wasn't supposed to enhance it.

This racket drove my pregnant wife mental. By the time she got out to the kitchen, all she saw was an empty pint glass and all she heard was Daft Punk. I tried to explain what I was doing. She walked over to the window, opened it from the side, not the top as I had done, and kicked them off. 'You don't even know how to open a f##king window?'

I didn't know it opened from the side – how was I to know?

She pounded back to bed and I was left sitting on the floor, pondering my protective abilities. There I sat, terrified, for almost two hours. What if I'm incapable of protecting my family? I thought. Am I ready to become a father? The more I thought about it, the more I reaffirmed my stance that I'd done the right thing. The cat wasn't doing anything to hurt us. He and his multiple sexual partners liked our bizarre concrete sex shelter, and the drinks, and especially the music. I had not alone protected my family, but I had also created the first ever liberal-sex cat disco. I'd created a home outside the home, a welcoming environment for randy cats. But here's a warning. Don't wake your pregnant wife at 4:30 a.m. to tell her that. When a heavily pregnant woman is screaming at you, 'Stop talking about cats!', it's time to sleep in the spare room. I realised that night that it's not intruders I need to worry about, it's me. And never, ever, ever, ever wake a pregnant woman to talk about cats.

11. His lists are useless. 'Leave out the bins' is not a life priority.

Some people are obsessed with making lists. My wife is one of these people. Too often I hear her shout in frustration at me: 'How do you get anything done?' Simple – I remember things. Okay, I forget some things, like pick-up times, doctors' appointments, nothing major. Besides, forgetting things allows us to live in relative freedom. If, say, the Romans hadn't forgotten to defend Rome from the Huns, I'd be speaking Latin and wearing a toga now, and I'd be freezing, because Dublin is always cold. I know this is a massive stretch and historically inaccurate, but I don't care. I don't like lists. List are made by two types of people: Very Organised People (like my wife) and Extremely Disorganised People, who generally get other people to do their lists for them (like me, or the Kardashians). Lists bother me. They bother me because they prioritise things.

Every person who makes a list puts the most important thing at the top, FACT. When I see people make lists in meetings, especially bosses, I automatically think, 'Who's on the top of that list?' I have a genuine fear of my name being on a list or, worse, not on a list. While I was waiting to be seated at a restaurant recently, a waitress with the attitude of a thousand pissed-off pubescents half-glanced at the side of my face and said with immense happiness, 'You're not on the list.' Nothing screams more directly into your soul than somebody saying, 'You're not on the list.' They might as well pull your trousers down, shout out your bank balance and declare, 'This man is a failure, everybody. Look at the failure – he has a tiny penis and he's not on the list.'

I also hate hearing 'There's a list going around' or 'You'd better get your name on the list' or, the mantra of most of my friends, who are trying to get their children into primary schools, 'You've to put your name down on the waiting list.' In Ireland, when you're born, they might as well just put your name down on a list for everything. In fact, our motto should be 'Ireland – Are you on the list?' So, for you list-obsessed people out there, I say no. For you are what I like to call Long-Finger Merchants. Oh, you 'didn't get around to it' but it's on your list? Well, that's exactly the same as me saying I didn't get around to it because I never once thought about doing whatever the stupid task was in the first place. Same result.

My wife buys lots of notebooks and guess what? They're full of … lists. She recently wrote down a list of 'life priorities':

* Make more time for the kids. Do something special with them every day
* Make more time for friends
* Get more sleep
* Go back running
* Prepare at least three healthy meals a week for kids
* Start weaning myself off sugar

So I wrote down mine:

* Fix Netflix or download *Paw Patrol*
* Get bin liners
* Leave out the bins
* Defuse atomic weapon in North Korea
* Get laptop fixed – take it back out of the bin
* Buy giant chocolate bar so kids don't eat it all

Now, you could look at these and think that Lorna and I have entirely conflicting priorities and that we're totally mismatched, and you'd be right. So what's the issue? Is my wife more concerned with our family? Yes. Has she a broader perspective on the grand plan of life? Yes. Is she a fully rounded person who sees friendship and family as the key to happiness? Yes. Will she be happier? No. Why? Because she made the stupid list.

If you want to live a happy life, STOP MAKING LISTS. If you want to live a life where adventure is around every corner (because you forgot to book a hotel room for your holidays) or big surprises come out of the blue, or your house magically turns into a semi-deflated paddling pool overnight (because you forgot to fix the boiler), don't make lists.

Here's my list on how to stop making lists:

* Nothing is a priority except telly and chips
* The kids will eventually tell you when they need their shots
* All household appliances eventually fix themselves over time
* Happiness is a myth – eat a bun
* Leave the bins out

To be a successful human being, all you have to do is make sure you remember to leave the bins out. What about shopping lists? Every Google page on how to shop effectively says make sure to make a list, or you'll end up buying unwanted items. On my gallant return from most hunting expeditions, Lorna will always moan that

* I didn't get nappies
* I didn't get milk
* I didn't get anything for the kids' lunches
* We don't need another Allen key set or organic smoked mackerel

This is always followed up by 'You never get what I asked you for, because you never make a list.' I never make a list because I care too much about the economy. Yes, the economy. If we all made lists before we went to the shops, we wouldn't buy stuff we don't need. Well, guess what? When you buy that stuff, it puts food on the table of the people who make it. What would have happened last year if I hadn't bought the organic oak-smoked mackerel fillets that I never ate? I tell you what would have happened ...

The following story is a dramatisation of events that never happened because I was a hero.

It's nearly time for the nine o'clock news and little Bobby's dad hasn't returned from the organic smoked mackerel factory yet. His mother tells him everything will be okay. She brushes his thick blond hair with her gentle hand and tells him that he should go to bed, so he can be up early in the morning.

'But what if Dada doesn't get his annual bonus, Mama?

Then we shan't be able to go to Tuscany on our holidays and we'll be forced to holiday at home.'

'Don't be silly,' his mother replies. 'Now off to bed with you,' but she knows something is wrong.

Little Bobby is brought up the stairs by Maria, the live-in au pair. She tells him everything will be okay and asks him another innocent question to see if he actually saw her and his father in the conservatory two weeks ago.

At eleven, the Range Rover pulls into the yard. It's JJ. He enters the marble-laden kitchen. His wife is waiting for him. 'There's something wrong, isn't there?' she says.

He looks at her, takes a deep breath and launches into a terrifying divulgence. 'The organic smoked mackerel section is f##ked. It didn't sell enough. All it needed was one overweight culchie to buy it in the west Dublin area. Just one delusional man with a bad BMI score to buy just one package. I thought it would appeal to people who felt guilty about ordering takeaway chips and who thought that they could balance out their calorie intake by eating this shit, but no.'

'What does this mean, JJ?' She is now in hysterics.

'It means ...' He falls to one knee. 'We're going to have to holiday in ... Wexford.'

She screams at him. 'WEXFORD? ARE YOU OUT OF YOUR F##KING MIND, JJ?'

'Keep it down, you'll wake Bobby and Maria ... is Maria here?' There is silence. He looks at her. 'We could always do a cheap two weeks in Portugal.' She throws the wine in his face and walks out the back door.

Upstairs, little Bobby is weeping as Maria tries to comfort him. 'I am from Portugal, Bobby, it's nice there,' she whispers.

Little Bobby draws in his breath. 'But Mama can't get a decent red there and she gets so angry.'

Maria hugs him tight and stares into his deep blue eyes and gently says, 'Do you play in the conservatory sometimes, Bobby?'

See, Lorna? That could have happened if I hadn't bought those organic smoked mackerel fillets that I never ate. And why didn't it happen? Because I didn't make a list. Thus, I am a hero.

12. He let our daughter, Olivia, ruin our lovely new couch with a tin of tomatoes.

Nothing highlights the way in which a long-term relationship develops like the deterioration of your couch. When we first moved into our two-bed flat, we bought what my wife called 'a little two-seater'. We'd cuddle up and look at our clean, clutter-free living room, watching programmes like *The News* or *Frasier*. Now, I look at the medieval battlefield that is our couch, strung with bloodstain-resembling juice drinks, mushed banana and the mildly bacterial excretions of a toddler. We've had it cleaned twice, but still, our two- and four-year-old decide to battle on it continuously and leave it looking like the aftermath of a music festival every evening. I swear I've found yoghurt pots there that are so old I've had conversations with them.

Our first mistake with our sofa came when we renovated our house. Trying to buy or even rent a house in Dublin in the last five to seven years has become near impossible. There are rumours that the next person who does it might win the Nobel Prize or be asked to do a Ted Talk. We were lucky.

We just managed to buy a nice three-bed semi-d in a lovely neighbourhood. However, it needed work. Having finished renovations, we then needed furniture. So every Saturday myself, Lorna and our daughter, Olivia, would trek along to furniture shops, along with thousands of other couples who looked exactly like us, to be laughed at.

Why? We'd see a couch we'd like. Then we would see if we could get a loan or finance to buy it. Sounds simple, yeah? Taking a massive leap into a fiscal furniture Funderland, we'd say to the salesman, 'We'll take it,' only to be greeted with derision. They would take great pride in saying, 'That will take eight weeks to build and ship and six days to deliver' or 'That's discontinued and it's sold and even if I could sell it to you, you'd have to go on a seven-year waiting list.' We became fed up with the whole process, which is fine if you're trying to buy a coffee grinder, but we needed somewhere to sit.

Eventually, on one of our expeditions, we saw a couch we liked. We made enquiries and it was for sale. It was an L shape, which we wanted, and it was just within our budget. We pounced and purchased. The shop sold and delivered. That evening, myself and Lorna just gazed at it. Our first piece of furniture. Having grown up a Catholic, I felt that we should call the local priest and have it blessed. This is something my wife and most of my friends think is hilarious. Even though I'm not religious, I still get the priest in my home town to bless my car when I buy a new one.

The first time Olivia asked me what God was, I was completely thrown. I tried to tell her 'it' was a person, who some people believe is looking over them and helping them.

She instantly said, 'So, it's like Nana when she's not up here with us?'

'Exactly,' I replied. 'Exactly.' When my father died, she asked me if he was 'up in the clouds with holy God.' Instead of getting into a deep philosophical debate with her, I said yes. She replied, 'So Granddad John in Limerick [Lorna's dad] is the only granddad left on the floor?' I love that: 'left on the floor'. If you're reading this, you're one of the lucky ones 'left on the floor'.

I've made a note of some of Olivia's questions, knowing that they'd come in handy some day. It's a list, but one I'd actually like to remember, because it's a reminder of how new everything is to a four-year-old.

Questions Olivia has asked me:
Why does the wind come on its own?
Why is the baby eating Mammy?
Where did yesterday go?
Why do the leaves colour themselves in?
Why do our legs move forward?
Why do people mix up numbers?
Why don't all cars move fast?
Why do they ask me where I'm from and not where I am?
If we're all going the same way, why are people asking where it is?
Why doesn't the wall fall down when I kick the ball really hard against it?
How do you remember?
If we can't see it, why is it there?
Why does the moon come out in the day but the sun doesn't come out at night?
Why does the night come?
Where does the sun go down to?
Why can't it be any day I want it to be?
Where do you get money?
What do teenagers do?

Anyway, back to the couch.

We sat on it. We took pictures of us sitting on it. I even began to think that the couch reflected my personality: sleek design, sharp lines, with a subtle natural grey fabric. Hold on a second, did I say fabric? Oh, yes, I did. Being first-time parents, we made the novice mistake of BUYING A FABRIC COUCH. Within forty minutes of the couch being in our house, Olivia had written all over it with crayon. Red wax and subtle grey fabric don't mix. Frantically trying to wash it off with soda water and spit, our flank was left open and a strawberry was launched into the armrest by a two-year-old grubby paw. We gave out to her, but at that age you might as well be talking to a two-year-old.

The damage was done. We stood back and gazed on our symbol of hope. Destroyed by a one-woman army of smudge. I fully understood my mother's cry of years before, 'I can't have anything nice in this house with ye.' Over the following weeks, the more experienced chimps of the commuter jungle would bombard us with the well-known mantra: 'Buy a leather couch.' Well, it was too late. We'd spent our money. Each day, our beautiful couch would look more like the arse end of the Lascaux caves. We would try to clean, but it was like presenting a blank canvas to Monet, and, my God, Olivia made some incredible impression on that couch.

One day, while cooking a spaghetti dish, I opened a can of tomatoes. Olivia had started moving chairs around the house and climbing up on them to reach higher items. We would normally hear the screeching of a chair, like the music in *Jaws*, and this would throw us into defence mode to stop her getting her hands on things. Not this day.

I was emptying the bins and came back into the kitchen. I looked around for the can of tomatoes, but couldn't find them. I knew something was wrong. In every person's life there is one moment when they know something bad has happened without even having to see it. You are rooted to the spot. You generally look down. Your brain isn't reacting. You are already moving to stage two, comprehending how to fix the impending disaster, even before it's happened. I turned my head. Sweet Jesus. Olivia had unleashed hell upon what had been, until thirty seconds previously, a grey couch. She had managed to mush an entire can of tomatoes into it in under half a minute.

She tried to explain to me she was helping me to cook. What? Spaghetti à la sofa? More important, Lorna would just ask why I'd left the can within her reach. It took four washes to get the stains out and the sprinkling of two bottles of unwanted aftershave on it to get rid of the odour of tinned tomato. Our house smelled like the front section of Boots for half a year.

It was then that we shamefully became 'throw people'. What are 'throw people'? For years, I would visit friends who had kids and wonder why they always had blankets thrown everywhere. (What really makes me scared is when you visit friends who don't have kids yet and they have throws everywhere. What the hell are they hiding?) I was even more confused by shops with sections fully dedicated to selling these blankets. What is their purpose? Their purpose is to hide our shame. Throws of Shame. Hiding the grubby imprint of our offspring, luring you to sit just millimetres away from what could be an Ebola outbreak. A house full of throws is a residence of surrender. Instead of waving a white flag, you throw blankets on your inability to control your tainted, contagious toddlers. It gets worse. When you start having to put throws on top of throws, you might as well live in a ditch. We learned the hard way. Buy a leather couch that's wipeable.

But I've found throws of shame extremely useful in other ways – life-changing, in fact.

Every relationship has its ups and downs, or as I like to call it, 'long passages of time where my wife hates me'. When we come to an impasse, I just say, 'Let's put a throw over it.' For example, I was supposed to come home early every Tuesday to let Lorna go to her DIY course; I forgot three or four times. When I got given out to, I'd just say, 'Put a throw over it.' I forgot to bring Tadhg to get his eyes tested? 'Put a throw over it.' Finally, I forgot Lorna's birthday backwards. That is, I celebrated it a day early with the kids. Yes, she was upset, but guess what? I told her to put a throw over it. In fact, I know that in almost every aspect of my relationship I'm pretty terrible, but it doesn't matter because I can put a throw over it. Like a child who covers their eyes and pretends nobody can see them, the adult equivalent is putting a throw over it. So, the next time your partner says that you're useless and a liability, tell them you love them and say with authority, 'We can put a throw over it.'

13. He shops for my Christmas present at 4:45 p.m. on Christmas Eve.

Along with my wife's intense obsession with candles, cushions and lamps, her feelings about fireplaces and sitting by the fire are unsettling. I swear, if she could train the fireplace to take out the bins once a week, she would have married it. Her most cherished memories of childhood are of sitting in the cosy warmth of the fire at Christmas. We both have memories of our mothers drying our hair by the fire after our baths. She remembers the night of her fifth birthday, getting into a new pair of pyjamas by the family fire, and I have a vivid memory of my mother warming my PJs by the fire, the night of my eighteenth birthday. I get it. Fire good. Cold bad.

Lorna now lights the fire regularly in our house. This does my head in, for two reasons. (1) Our house, unlike houses in the eighties, is insulated, so, regardless of what the weather is like outside, the house gets too warm; and (2) she never cleans it out. I'm always left cleaning out the fireplace and I hate doing it. It is the one job that reminds me what most Irish houses were like when I was growing up. The eighties didn't need *Dynasty* or shoulder pads: it needed adequate central heating.

There was a solution, however. A dangerous, terrible solution.

When I was growing up, our house always had more water on the inside of the windows than on the outside. Most Irish builders thought ventilation was the British political policy towards Northern Ireland and that insulation was something you'd get off rabbits or badgers. Every school morning I'd wake up and I'd run downstairs and straight towards the Superser that my mother had put in the middle of the kitchen. If I tried to get dressed anywhere else in the house, hypothermia would set in. I once tried putting on my shirt in the bedroom and I lost a finger.

Mention 'Superser' to anyone born after 1986 and they think it's a massive teacher or a drug bought in a head shop. For those of you who were lucky enough to grow up in an economy, let me explain what a 'Superser' is, or, hopefully someday, was. A 'Superser' was basically a rectangular metal box that, when in the mood, doubled up as a gas heater. By 'heater' I mean as in scalding, scorched eyebrows and gas, as in 'I can smell gas.' A yellow cylinder full of the stuff would be attached to a nozzle and placed inside the metal death-trap. You would then willingly allow the beautiful natural gas to flow out into the room. But it was totally safe, because the gas would then be ignited by pressing down frantically on a tiny plastic button attached to a spark plug, which would in turn light up three cheese graters on the front of the box. These would throw off the equivalent heat of a two-year-old clapping their hands. Simple, brilliant technology, but there was a catch! The tiny plastic button that ignited the gas never worked. So what did thousands of Irish people do to ignite the fiery embers of Supersers across the land? We lit a baton of rolled-up newspaper from the cooker, released the gas and tried to stick the baton through the hurling-helmet guard in front of the cheese graters. This would supposedly protect you from the resulting engulfment by ferocious blue flames. This ritual consistently burned my mother's hair every morning. Sometimes, I didn't know whether to call the fire brigade or eat my corn flakes.

The catch phrase in our house was 'Close the door,' followed by 'YOU'RE LETTING THE HEAT OUT.' This was repeated in nearly every house on our road. From an early age we were trained in how to enter a room without even opening a door. David Copperfield visited our house several times to see how I did it, but I would never reveal my secret. The heat was treated like an elusive spy who would cunningly try to escape out of a room any way possible and head off to London to buy forbidden things, like condoms or mint Kit-Kats.

I remember one viciously cold night counting how many times my parents said, 'Close that f##king door.' The final tally was close to three hundred.

As if the danger of leaving a door open or lighting a Superser wasn't petrifying enough, we had a heating system in our house called The Pump. Most houses on our road didn't have oil or gas heating; they were heated with solid fuel, mostly coal, wood and turf. There was one house, about thirty miles away, that had a thermostat. We went there once on our school tour instead of to the sugar beet factory in Carlow. There are two major problems with solid fuel: (1) it's dirty; (2) there is no way of controlling the temperature of the radiators or the water. There is a (3), but this was still long before anybody cared about climate change. In fact, if any country in the world could benefit from global warming, it would be Ireland. I have a dream that one day we'll all be able to eat ice cream … outside.

In every house, there was a massive copper cylinder full of water. This tank got its own room. Our family called it 'the cubby hole'. In every other village, town, city and county it was called 'the hot press' or, if you were posh, 'the airing cupboard'. The first time I moved in with Lorna I told her that I'd put my tool box in her cubby hole. When she replied, 'I'm not into that,' I said, 'Okay. Well, can I put it under the sink?' It took a frank and honest discussion to eventually iron out my simple mistake.

When you lit a fire in the fireplace or cooker, it would heat a back burner that would heat the water that, in turn, would pump hot water into the radiators to heat the house. Simple, except for one problem. How did you know when the water was boiled? You had to listen for it. That's right, you had to listen for the tank to make some grumbling noises and when it did, you had to race as fast as possible to switch on 'the pump'. If you didn't switch it on in time, the cylinder would expand with steam and explode. Basically, everybody in Ireland had a bomb in their house. I'd often be walking home from school and see houses flying through the air. Ah, they didn't get to the pump in time, I'd think. Every time I see an open fire, I think, 'They'd better listen out for the pump,' and 'I'll have to clean that out in the morning.' Thus, I don't like open fires: they're too much work compared to the alternative: pressing a button on our smartphones to heat the house.

My wife's solution to what she calls my 'odd and twisted way of thinking' was simple. She told me she wanted an ash vacuum cleaner for Christmas. First, I didn't think such a thing existed and, second, buying your wife a vacuum cleaner, unless that vacuum cleaner can bring her places that I, or her framed picture of John Hamm, can't, is not a good idea. I parked her idea. In fact, I parked it so far back that it took until Christmas Eve 2017 for it to rear its head again.

In a blind panic, I bought my wife jewellery on 24 December that year for Christmas. It wasn't as if I didn't have enough time to buy her a more thoughtful gift; it's just that I love the pulsating blind-panic feeling I give myself every year around Christmas. Some people are extraordinarily well prepared, for example my wife. She will have bought every present that's required for Christmas, and some spares, long before the big day. In fairness to her, she puts both our names on the gifts, thus making me look good. Every year, she tells me specifically what she wants, then I forget what she's asked for and end up running around a shopping centre on Christmas Eve.

This is how every Christmas morning goes with my wife:

Me: Wow, thanks, that's such a good present. Now open yours.
Lorna opens present.
Lorna: Why did you get me a microscope?
Me: I thought you said you wanted one?
Lorna: No, I told you to get me a hair dryer or a spa voucher. *You* wanted the microscope.
Me: Oh.

I was adamant that this Christmas, Christmas 2017, was going to be different. I wanted to buy Lorna a present that said, 'I love you; I can't thank you enough for our children and for all the sacrifices you make.' So I ran into a jewellery shop in a shopping centre on Christmas Eve and bought her earrings, or a bracelet, I can't remember which. Along with all the other men in the queue, I smugly purchased a gift that I have been brainwashed over the years into thinking is a girl's best friend. I'm not the most woke man in the world, but I'm pretty sure that wine and an endless supply of batteries is.

Happy with my gift, I texted her. *Got your gift.*

The reply came back as I was walking to my car. *Thanks – as long as it's not jewellery. You know I can't wear it. You didn't have to get me anything.* In that moment, I realised that because I'd bought her jewellery, effectively, I hadn't got her anything.

I ran into Argos. 'Sorry, we're shut,' said the drained teenage member of staff, who looked like she'd just been through a hostage negotiation. I ran, and I mean ran, to the large department store called House of Fraser. 'Sorry, son, we're closed,' said a security guard. I pelted around the vast, squeaky marble floors, all four levels of them, to try and find any shop that was open to get my wife a present, but no joy. I eventually gave up and decided to google 'shops open now'. Everything seemed shut. I got into my car and drove to another shopping centre off Dublin's M50 motorway. Everything was shut there too. Shop workers laughed as they walked with their co-workers to the pub. They had no idea of my quandary.

I drove out through the myriad roundabouts, all decorated with lights and reindeer. Normally, I'd drive home on the M50 but I decided to go back home the long way instead, through all the suburbs.

Being from the country, you never think that cities are made up of villages. Because the urban landscape seems so vast, you never think that the local spirit exists. But driving home through all the swallowed-up villages, I saw people outside their local churches and each little group reminded me that it doesn't matter where you're from, because … Hold that thought. In fact, forget that nostalgic drivel … There was a shop open! A small hardware store was open, selling solid fuel and big tinfoil baking trays for the turkeys.

I walked in and it was mostly full of older ladies buying bales of briquettes and bags of coal. I walked along its two little dusty aisles, looking at silicone piping, grout, washers and duct tape. I thought, this is useless, I can't buy her angle-grinder plates or a spanner set, but then, lo and behold, there at the back of the shop in beautiful yellow plastic and metal, was the most gorgeous apparition I'd ever seen … an ash vacuum cleaner. I knelt before it. I gave thanks to it. For here lay the true saviour of Christmas.

When I went to buy it, the man behind the counter told me that it was a display model and that he could order me a new one. I told him, 'I don't care if it displays psychotic tendencies, I'll take it,' and, for basically the first time in human history, I asked a man on Christmas Eve if he could gift-wrap an ash vacuum cleaner for me. He couldn't. Instead he wrapped it in newspaper and black insulation tape. Beggars can't be choosers, I thought.

For once, I'd actually bought my wife exactly what she wanted for Christmas. When I got home, everybody was in bed. I went to leave my present under the tree, but it wouldn't fit, so I put it in the middle of the kitchen. I sat down to watch some telly and fell asleep on the couch.

* * *

'SANTA HAS COME!' screamed my daughter. It was 6 a.m. and I had slept the whole night in my clothes on the couch. Lorna, our kids and her family were now all in our sitting room, watching the magical moment of toddlers ripping apart wrapping paper like ravenous hyenas. Lorna handed me my gift. She'd got me exactly what I asked for: two replacement cylinders for my SodaStream and a tiny Swiss penknife that had a tiny scissors and a tiny nail file.

When everybody had finished opening their gifts, the only thing left was the monolith I'd left in the kitchen. 'Mammy, open your present!' the kids screamed.

Lorna was intrigued. She began to tear the newspaper off, little by little, and then the hyenas joined in, until they'd stripped it down to the large Ruhr Valley cardboard box.

'What is it?' she said.

'You'll have to open the box as well.' I was so happy.

She started to pull out the fake yellow straw and poly board that protected it until she finally realised what it was. She turned to me and said, so lovingly, 'You got me a f##king vacuum cleaner?'

'Yeah,' I chirped. 'That's exactly what you asked me for.'

The look on her face was reminiscent of a puppy's when it has just been told that it it's going back to the pound. I tried to argue that it was exactly what she wanted. Her family looked at me with disgust, but said things like 'It's a very practical gift' and 'It's always nice to get something you'll use.'

I ran out to the car and got the jewellery. When I came back in, I declared, 'Only messing, here's your real present.'

She opened it and said, 'You know I don't wear jewellery, Bernard. Look, it's okay, I didn't want anything.'

I should have left it but, of course, I didn't. I replied, 'You're as odd as two left feet. Every woman likes jewellery, except you.' Again, I could have left it there but, oh no. I went on, 'This is your favourite present – being able to say I didn't get you anything.' I could have most definitely stopped at that, but now my mouth had taken over Government Buildings and was issuing press statements: 'You asked for the vacuum cleaner. I got it for you.'

And then, the *pièce de resistance.* 'You're so ungrateful.'

It was now official. I'd started a row on Christmas Day. It's a tradition in nearly every house, but I wish it hadn't been in our house that morning. Hours passed and we still hadn't spoken. Then, during the afternoon, I had a brainwave. I lit the fire. Eventually, we all sat down at it. We played board games and, later on that night, put the kids into their new pyjamas. I could see that Lorna was happy. More important, I could see what she was trying to do. She was recreating those special memories for our kids that she'd had as a child.

When we went to bed my wife eventually broke the silence. She looked me in the eye and said, 'You can clean out the fire in the morning, Bernard. You can use your new f##king vacuum cleaner.' Maybe I did get her the present she wanted after all. The present of me doing something for the rest of my life that she knows I hate doing. Surely that's what love, and Christmas, is really all about.

14. He's obsessed with fads, but sticks with nothing, so the house is littered with things he no longer uses.

Lorna's right – I'm a terrible man for the fads. I try out a new one nearly every week, from meditation to drinking apple cider vinegar to walking backwards to fix my posture. If it promises to make me slimmer, I'll try anything. Nowadays, my fads are generally driven by social media clickbait, but I grew up reading women's magazines. The first fad I ever tried was from an old *Cosmo* I stole from my sister. It recommended getting rid of acne by washing your face with olive oil soap. Having acne, but no olive oil soap, I washed my face in Crisp 'n Dry … it made it worse.

Having three older sisters had some benefits, though, mostly plenty of trashy reading material. What strikes me is that the same articles pop up time and time again: how to lose weight and how to please your man in the bedroom. I've never seen an article that gets to the heart of the latter. I know how to please a woman in the bedroom: you don't snore, wake her, or hog the duvet. However, that wouldn't make for an entertaining or salacious *Cosmo* cover story.

I've constantly wondered why I am obsessed with quick fixes. I know from having lost weight before that it was because of diet and a bit of exercise. I know from being unhappy with my looks that when I'm more attentive with my grooming and clothes, it can make a massive difference. So why all the quick fixes? Because I'm not a consistent person and because I hate moderation. I'm flighty. A little quick fix or fad here and there subdues me into to thinking that I'm on the right track. As for moderation, we all know it's the key to maintaining a healthy life, but it's so boring.

As a Catholic, I don't do moderation. The Pope didn't ask Michelangelo to whitewash the Sistine Chapel ceiling, oh no. Instead, it took twenty years of pain and death. Also, as Catholics, we're taught to pray for things if we run out. For instance, my wife would always give out to me for eating the entire pack of biscuits once opened, leading to her hiding her treats in various places around the house. She always says, 'Why don't you leave some for tomorrow? You'll have nothing then.' To which I always say a little prayer: 'Dear Lord, I've eaten all the Jammie Dodgers. Will you please replace them tomorrow as I will forget to go to the shop? Amen.' That's how Catholicism works for me.

My wife also reminds me daily of all the fads I've started but never continued. For example: *Running in water for my knee*: I had to stop because people were looking at me nearly drowning in the deep end. *Pilates*: I had to stop because I kept breaking wind in the classes. The other students were calling me the 'fart guy'. *Baking*: Both of us were, and still are, obsessed with *The Great British Bake-off*. It inspired me to bake. My wife bought me a professional mixer. I had an apron and everything. I was going to become a baker. Unfortunately, measurement is not my thing. I destroyed our oven and clogged its fan by using fifteen times the recommended amount of baking soda trying to make, and I quote: 'a rustic Irish loaf'. *Kettle bells*: I kept this going for years, until I broke the ceiling in our flat by throwing the bell over my head. *Road cycling*: I initially loved this. I had all the Lycra gear, the Italian bike and the clip-on shoes. However, I did make a total idiot of myself at the traffic lights in a busy junction, when I tried to clip out my foot and got stuck in the pedal. I crashed onto the road. An old lady with one of those carrier bags on wheels helped me up eventually.

However, the longest fad I took part in – and Lorna still slags me off about it to this day – is triathlons. Yes, like most men of my age, I became completely obsessed with them. However, on my first and last attempt at one, I accidentally (genuinely) cut the running course short and finished in an incredible time. I was delighted with myself, until I was informed of the error. That was my only foray into triathlons. Oh, I forgot one thing. I give up on things a lot. In a world where we're told to keep persisting, I say no. I get fed up with something, I move on. Nobody gets hurt, except for my bank balance and, once, my weak digestive system.

Let me explain. It's to do with my teeth. I've never looked after them properly. My wife constantly gives out to me for not visiting the dentist regularly as dental cover costs us a fortune on our health insurance. But I don't care. As I've said, I have a fear of needles. It's so bad that I once tied a tooth that was killing me to a door handle and got my flatmate to slam it. Needless (no pun intended) to say, it didn't work. It resulted in a dentist having to pull the tooth out without anaesthetic, because I'd drunk a naggin of whiskey to dull the pain, so he couldn't administer one. In fact, nearly 99 per cent of my self-medicated adventures never work. Neither did my expedition into whitening my teeth by swallowing litres of coconut oil over a three-week period.

I was working on an Irish comedy programme called *The Republic of Telly* at the time. One of the guests was Amanda Byram, who presented *The Swan* and *Dancing with the Stars*, among various other programmes. During some downtime, I was talking about how I never smile because I'm self-conscious about my yellow teeth, but that the whitening strips and dentist tooth-whitening are too painful. She told me that I should do the ancient art of 'oil pulling'. This is where you get an oil (generally coconut oil) and swill it around your mouth for about 15 to 20 minutes a day. It's supposed to improve overall oral health and one of the benefits some people get is whiter teeth.

That evening I went into a chemist and bought a massive tub of coconut oil. Ready for my swilling voyage, I set sail. I began to do it every morning. After about two weeks, I noticed that it was actually working. My teeth were getting a little bit whiter but, more important, I stopped getting mouth ulcers. The world, as far as I'm concerned, is split into two kinds of people: those who get mouth ulcers and those who live without pain. I always get them when I'm under stress or have to speak at something. They are the worst little prickly bastard of a thing to suffer from, especially when it comes to eating, when they destroy all comfort. Small, painful and impossible to heal, they are the human equivalent of the thorn in the lion's foot. Now, thanks to my regular swilling, they were gone.

I started to bestow my new-found fad on everybody I knew. I was close to standing up on soap boxes and preaching its benefits in shopping centres, like a travelling salesman in the old American West selling 'Dr Bernardo's Miracle Cure

For All Ills'. I wanted to scream, 'Everybody, stop buying stuff you don't need – it won't fill the void. Just swill coconut oil every morning. You will be a different person within a week, or your money back.' I was a new man.

It was only in the third week that I started to feel a strong pain in my stomach.

It actually woke me up one night. Being a hypochondriac, this really rattled me. I tried to eat breakfast but couldn't: the pain was getting worse. That morning, I had a voiceover to record at 11 a.m. I thought, if I can get that done, I'll come home and go to the doctor if it still persists. I also did what I naturally always do and googled my symptoms. Having assured myself I had cancer, I set off to get the tram into town. After two stops, I was doubled over in pain. I had to get off at a stop called 'Windy Arbour', and how apt was the name of that stop.

When I got off the tram, I tried to stand up and when I did, I let off the biggest fart the world has ever heard, but hopefully not smelled. It was horrendous and lasted about two minutes. I was so worried about its ferocity, I tried staying away from open flames in case I started a fire. When my gaseous episode elapsed, I was pain-free. I could walk again and my stomach didn't feel like it was trying to digest an angle grinder. Delighted that my pain was only gas, I hopped on the next available tram and made my way into the city centre.

I sat down on a wet seat. I got back up, but the seat itself was bone dry. I went and sat on another seat. Same thing - it was wet. I got up, but that actual seat was dry, too. In fact, every seat I sat in was dry. It was then I realised that I was leaking. The coconut oil had built up in my body and started to gush out. I smelled like a tropical paradise, a seeping leaky-bum paradise.

I stood all the way into the city centre and eventually made it to a toilet in a coffee shop. Gallons of coconut oil were coming out of me. I tried to clean myself up as much as I could and made my way into a nearby shopping centre and bought a pair of tracksuit pants in a sports shop. I put my coconut-steaming jeans into a bag. Now, I was wearing shoes and a shirt with tracksuit bottoms. I looked like a guy who was anally leaking.

I got to the voiceover and asked if I could stand. Luckily for me, it only lasted ten minutes, but the engineer kept saying, 'Do you smell coconut?' For fear of leaking on a taxi or on public transport I walked the six miles home. I sat on newspaper for the rest of the day. My wife, then girlfriend, called over after work. I told her what had happened and her reply, as always, was succinct: 'You f##king idiot, you're not supposed to swallow it.' I had been rinsing, then swallowing coconut oil every morning. I must have gone through at least five jars of the stuff.

It took about ten hours for all the oil to come out. To this day, I can't touch the stuff. I used to enjoy the odd Bounty bar, but even that simple pleasure is gone. However, I rarely get mouth ulcers any more and my teeth got whiter. Life isn't a simple equation. Sometimes you have to have balance. Yes, I anally leaked coconut oil for a full day, but I have whiter teeth. And I am proud of myself, because unlike most of my other fads, it lasted a full three weeks. However, just be careful if you're ever on the Luas. Don't sit on a seat smelling of coconut.

15. He uses all my expensive skincare products and he thinks I don't know about it.

I learned the guitar when I was twelve. I was given one for Christmas. By the time I was thirteen, three months later, I was playing it three or four nights a week with my dad in various pubs and halls. My father wasn't a rocker: he played the accordion for Irish dancing céilís, sometimes with a singer, who would generally perform traditional songs. When you're thirteen, playing traditional music is a highway to being ripped apart by your peers at school. Luckily, when I was a teenager, Irish music was not seen as 'cool' exactly, but had slipped its way silently into the 'alright' category, mostly thanks to *Riverdance*. However, let's just say no one ever does 'air-accordion' as a solo, and I don't recall Oasis or Blur having an accordion player in their bands.

I learned very quickly. My father was a little bit impatient, so if you wanted to play something, you'd better know it. Looking back now, it was the best training you could ever get. I never studied music, but I can pretty much play anything – that's what playing three to four hours a night at nearly a thousand gigs will give you. Talent is overrated; doing something for a thousand hours isn't.

We would pack the car at 6:30 in the evening and head off, mostly to hotel function rooms on weekdays and pubs on the weekends, putting up and down equipment, getting lost en route (no satnavs) and having rows that the Gallagher brothers or the Ramones would be squeamish of.

I remember one night we were heading to a gig in a hotel in Kilkenny. My father's favourite thing ever was to drive off as you were trying to get into the car. It made him laugh until he wet himself. He started doing this as we were trying to get out of the driveway of our house. I was a poster child for puberty, spotty and boiling over with a delicate consommé of hormones. I lashed out and ran at the car. The result? He drove over my foot.

I was screaming in pain. This got him pretty worked up. I was roaring, 'You drove over my foot.'

'No I didn't, you walked underneath the wheel.' This went on for a while. After sitting in a corner for a few minutes, sulking, I got into the car. By the time we took off, it was forgotten. What you have to remember is that when you're in a band, even if it's with your dad, the gig goes on, with or without the use of your foot. And that's what it was like. It was tough going for what was very little money, but I loved it.

Dad bought me my first proper guitar. It's the instrument I still have to this day. I slept with it. I brought it to school. I never studied for an exam; I just played that guitar. I knew every Oasis, Beatles and Blur song. I would learn anything I heard with a guitar in it, even advertisements. I was in a school band and we – well, I should say I – called it The Plebs. The other lads never really signed off on that one. I dreamed that I would become a rock star, but it's hard when you have thick red hair and the looks of a vitamin D-deprived leprechaun. And when most of your 'gigs' revolve around knowing the chord progression to polkas, reels, hornpipes and 'Danny Boy'.

A lot of folk-music guitarists use a finger-picking style. To do this, you can either use finger picks, which you attach to your fingers, or grow your nails. I chose the latter, as the finger picks kept cutting off the blood supply to my fingers. Growing your nails is a lot harder than you'd imagine, so you'd think most women, especially those who keep their nails well, would be supportive, but no. Women would constantly look at my right hand quizzically. 'Your nails are disgusting,' a date once told me. Trying to explain to her why I needed them, she just told me that it looked like I was using them to pleasure myself.

However, what is most unhelpful is that my nails keep breaking. I've tried every supplement and all the go-to foods that are supposed to make them stronger, but nothing works. My wife, who also hates them, suggested that I should make an appointment with a nail bar. More nail bars have probably sprung up in Dublin over the last ten years than actual bars, so I got her to make an appointment for me. I was planning on getting something called 'clear shellac' nails. 'They will never break,' Lorna assured me.

When I showed up at the nail bar, they asked me several questions. I was the only man they had ever had in their shop and they were intrigued as to why I wanted false nails. After I told them, they asked me to sit in the window. Confession time here: I'm not the world's most modern man. I know I shouldn't give a shit if someone sees me getting my nails done, but I'm sorry, I'm not sitting in the shop window of a nail salon on a busy city-centre street. Why do massage parlours and hairdressers do this? At what stage do they think, 'I know people can feel vulnerable when they're getting cosmetic procedures done, so to calm them down, let's put them in the front window so that every passer-by can look in at them and, hopefully, judge them.' I declined the appointment, making up a ridiculous excuse. I said that I'd just remembered that I didn't have the self-confidence to become a hand model today. Instead, I went home and while my wife was at work, I raided her medicine cabinet to see if she had any ideas in her treasure trove of pharmaceutical purchases.

Every man uses his partner's products, but the lies about it! It's a Pandora's box of intrigue. I got caught once using Crème de la Mer on a dry rash I had on my arse. Lorna screamed at me, 'That's a hundred and twenty euros, Bernard!' As the row continued, all I could think was, 'Who pays €120 for arse cream?'

After that, she started to hide the good stuff elsewhere. My raids went on unabated. Now, I found a bottle labelled 'clear nail varnish'. I tried it on my nails and it was good. It definitely hardened them up, but it was too shiny and not strong enough. I dripped loads of it all over the sink and cleaned it up with toilet paper. Like a lot of humanity's most treasured inventions, my next discovery was an accident. I noticed that the toilet paper soaked up the nail varnish and created a perfect substance, light but hard. I fashioned five nails from it by peeling toilet paper in half and soaking it in the varnish. I moulded the toilet-paper nails on my fingers but they wouldn't stay on. So I bought super glue and glued them on, while also hardening the clear varnish with a hair dryer. It was only when I had them glued on that I realised they were too thick and that they looked really odd. The kind of odd that would make you think I was Dracula, trying to loosen up and let a five-year-old make my hands.

But then I realised I couldn't do anything with my right hand. Everything I went to pick up became a spatial awareness test, and I couldn't type. I eventually went into a hardware store and bought sandpaper and sanded them down. That night, when Lorna came home, I successfully hid my right hand. She went to bed before me and I got in to bed long after she had fallen asleep.

Apparently, in my sleep, I spoon the duvet. Lorna constantly pulls the duvet back off me. This goes on all night, apparently, but I'm oblivious, as I'm a heavy sleeper. However, this time, in one of my wife's more boisterous duvet landgrabs, she did untold damage. My nail got stuck in the duvet cover, so, when she pulled it, she pulled my index fingernail off as well.

I woke screaming. The pain was insane. I've never felt more acute trauma in my life. My wife always says that nothing compares to childbirth. That's not true: getting a nail pulled off your finger is the equivalent of having triplets. There was blood everywhere. I explained to her what I'd done and we spent hours looking for my old nail to try and stick it back on. We eventually found the nail but the skin on my finger had closed up by that stage and I'm not sure if you can put them back anyway.

The following morning, I cleaned the bed, binned the sheets and Sellotaped my nail back onto my hand. It was ridiculously painful and I cancelled a gig I was supposed to do that night in Belfast, as every time I went to grip the steering wheel, the pain throbbed in my hand.

Yes, it was an idiotic thing to do, but you expect some sympathy from your partner; but when she got home from work, Lorna said, 'You're the only person I've ever known who's called in sick with a broken nail.'

16. He thinks he invented iced tea.

'm a ventor, not an inventor. That is, I can see and talk about my inventions, but that's where my *in*volvement, *in*spiration and *in*terest end. I can tell you about my inventions, I just can't show them to you, because I can't make them. When I've tried to make them, I've just ended up spending money that I don't have with no outcome.

My last invention revolved around weight loss. I've desperately tried to lose weight over the last twenty years. I first noticed a little belly appearing in college. It was an odd arrival on my torso – I had always been a scrawny child and teenager. Up until my mid-twenties, I never weighed more than twelve stone, but by my late twenties I was fat. It's a term I hate, 'fat'; but 'overweight' doesn't do it for me. Saying 'I'm overweight' sounds too medical for me, almost like it's something that has just happened to me, like flu, and the term does nothing to keep me going on my endless weight-loss journey. The word 'fat', albeit constantly used to fat shame and belittle people, describes exactly what I have. I'm not fat – I *have* fat. The word makes me want to fight it. Get rid of it off my body.

I never envisioned myself as being fat. I was so thin for the first half of my life that every piece of clothing had had to be taken in, but on my wedding day I was sixteen stone, an increase of four stone in seven years. How did it happen? The same way it happens to everybody. I, like millions of people on the planet, somehow ended up eating more and moving less. In the last decade I've tried everything. The Atkins diet made me constipated and sick of eating animals. Veganism was nice, but I truly got fed up with chopping vegetables and, my God, the farting. I have done most diets and one-on-one programmes, all the time knowing that I just had to stop putting food into my mouth.

If you cannot understand why people like me get fat, stop moving your hands. I said stop moving your hands. You will be able to do so for a few minutes, but eventually you'll have to get on with life. Your hands are like my stomach. I can stop it for a little while, but eventually it starts barking again and sugar and bread go in, because they are the simplest, quickest things to hand. I'd love to cook homemade meals and to enjoy warming soups and winter salads, but chocolate and white bread taste so f##king good.

There is research to suggest that cocaine is more addictive than sugar, so I tried to switch to cocaine for a while instead. It was all going fine until my self confidence rose so high that I started several media agencies and had no time for the kids or my wife any more (please note that this is a joke). I know there is no quick fix to weight loss but unlike others, I refuse to give my life over to moderation and the adage of 'eat less, move more'. I like to align myself with ancient alchemists. They tried for centuries to make gold from lead and rocks and hair, only to be either poisoned or to die due to failure.

It was with this spiritually and historically tempestuous sentiment that I decided to again forgo reason and science and try hypnotherapy. I've had quite a rough ride with hypnotherapy, especially in college, when a hypnotherapist convinced me that I was in the band B*Witched. I wore only denim for years after that.

The second time I was hypnotised was when my wife was expecting our first child. She decided to do a hypno-birthing course. At the end of the course, the instructor asked all of us to lie down on the floor. She brought us through some calming breathing techniques to help the men as well as the women through the birth. I fell asleep. My wife was mortified. She said while all the other men were trying to help their pregnant wives to their feet, I was actually snoring away on the ground and eventually went into the foetal position. I wasn't embarrassed because that's what the lady had told us to do: sleep. On the way home, Lorna was laughing about it, but I was delirious because here, for the first time in my life, something I would call 'hippy-dippy shite' had actually worked on me.

A few Google searches later (I'm working on a new book entitled *My Catastrophic Google Adventures*) I found out that you could do hypnotherapy for weight loss. Yes! I thought. Another distraction from 'eat less, move more'. I downloaded a hypnotherapy app onto my phone and relaxed into another hopeful quick-fix weight-loss journey.

At first, I noticed no difference with the hypnotherapy, but eventually found it made me sleep. So much so that whenever I felt I needed fifteen minutes, I'd just put on my earphones and I'd nod off. I was listening to it three times a day for a month and getting a little power nap each time. It had no effect on my waistline, but quite a radical effect on my hormones.

To say I was horny all the time would be very accurate. My wife found my amorous affections so much increased, she seriously considered getting a vet to neuter me. It was insane. I actually couldn't control myself. I felt like I'd transformed into a ginger werewolf with two penises. I started to run every day just to tire myself out and started lifting weights to take my mind off what was a constant 'awakening' problem down below.

One day, while I was doing my meditation, my wife went into our room and woke me. At this stage she was running away from me (we conceived our third child during this bizarre period). When I tried to get back into the hypnotherapy, I got the shock of my life. Instead of what I thought I'd been listening to, I was actually listening to 'You stand proud and erect, you are hard and inexhaustible, your engine is full of fire.' I was listening to a hypnotherapy session not for weight loss, but for 'increasing testosterone'. On further googling, I read that if you increase testosterone, it's proven to increase weight loss. I had to stop. It did work for me, just not for anybody else.

I needed an alternative, before I had to take the boring 'eat less, move more' voyage again. It came as a twofold annunciation one Saturday evening after a row over tea bags.

My wife doesn't drink tea, but she buys every conceivable herbal tea bag you can get off a supermarket shelf. She has the idea that because she hates tea and coffee, maybe she can enjoy a herbal tea. After a row over who clogs up space with more of their stuff, I went to the press. I took out the 22 boxes of herbal tea and declared to the house, 'I, Bernard O'Shea, did not buy these.' I know why she buys them, though. It's the same reason why I buy root ginger. I don't like it, but it's supposed to be nice and good for you and I have this vision of me curling up on a cold winter's day enjoying a nice tea with root ginger, knowing that I'm in control of my urges and not stuffing my face with Tunnock's tea cakes.

In fairness, her defence was that it was the only thing she had bought that was clogging up the tiny amount of press space in the kitchen. Nevertheless, it was a victory for me and they don't come too often, if ever. However, it was short lived, as she told me to 'throw them out'. Throw them out, I thought to myself. Why, that would be way too easy. There must be something I could do with them. It was another chance to invent.

I started to mix all the different herbal tea bags together to see which combination would taste the nicest. After three or four days, I had invented not just a new drink, but a new flavour of herbal tea. I mixed raspberry and mint with chamomile, fennel, forest berry and something called throat-ease. I threw in a regular Lyons tea bag and a spoon of honey and hey presto, I'd invented a new cold-tea drink that was going to topple the soft-drinks market. It was, in my opinion, delicious. Nobody else tasted it, so you will have to agree with me. The only downside was that in my exuberant need to use up all the tea bags, I had made about fifty pints of the stuff in the large silver Ikea bowls that we used to clean the baby bottles in. I'd got quite obsessed with Ikea and purchased fifteen of them one day. Another victory for me, as I exclaimed to the house again: 'You see, I told you they would come in handy.'

I couldn't keep them in the bowls for ever as my wife (who was offered a share in my business in exchange for helping me clean up the mess) told me to get rid of them. I bottled them, or should I say bagged them, in Ziploc bags and put them in the freezer. Each day I would drink a bag of my wonderful new drink, which I called 'Bernie's Secret' as it was a secret recipe.

It had a massive benefit: I started to lose weight. Every time I felt the need to eat, I would just sip away on a bag of my tea. The weight dropped off. There was only one problem: I had to bring it everywhere. Carrying bags of frozen tea is not easy. It melts and people look at you oddly on public transport if you're drinking a semi-frozen liquid out of a Ziploc bag.

I convinced myself that it wasn't water I was losing, but actual fat. I genuinely felt I had hit a magical combination, a weight-loss elixir for the modern age. I set aside a week and wrote up a *Dragon's Den* pitch. I dropped the name Bernie's Secret in favour of Fasten, as in to lose weight fast by drinking my tea. I made up a further fifty bottles of it to give out to people to test it until my wife pointed out the fatal flaw in my business. She said, 'What if it *is* diet and exercise and not the tea?'

'It's not diet and exercise, I replied, 'it's the tea.'

'Well,' she went on, 'you've been drinking it for three months. So if it's just the tea you'll have to get one person to drink two bottles a day for three months.'

'Yeah, but that's why I'll sell loads of it, because you'll have to buy two bottles a day.'

She then looked at my food diary, which I keep on my phone. 'You're dropping a meal because your stomach is full of water.'

I wasn't giving in. 'Maybe so, but it's the combination of diet and exercise *and* the tea.'

Then came the clanger that she has doled out at every opportunity to get a laugh. 'Bernard, are you seriously telling me that you've invented iced tea?'

I get so focused on doing something that it's all or nothing; it's never been about balance for me, ever. Balance bores me to death. I spent two weeks trying to drink as much of that tea as possible before eventually throwing it down the sink. It was disgusting, but it worked.

'You're right, it's iced tea,' I agreed.

Lorna started laughing at me. 'You are a total f##king idiot.'

'You're right, I am … I'll just have to go back to the hypnotherapy, won't I?'

There was silence, while she thought about the inconvenience of my ardour. 'Did you throw out all the tea?'

17. He can't follow simple instructions. It can't be that hard to order a Chinese takeaway.

My wife has a plain diet. I've only ever seen her order one thing from the Chinese takeaway and that's a '3 in 1'. For those of you who don't know this delicacy, a 3 in 1 is rice, chips and curry sauce served together in one tray. It is the one of those unique Irish–international carbohydrate meals. Another example would be lasagne with chips (the Italians think this is hilarious), or chips with mashed or boiled potatoes. Once, while on a family holiday I saw a man – definitely in his late 70s – order just a plate of potatoes in the hotel we were staying at. Funnily enough, that's what we'd ordered for our two-year old, Tadhg. Ah, the potato circle of life.

The 3 in 1 is something I thought every Chinese restaurant served. I never thought this unusual culinary treat would have got me into so much trouble with so many people in such a short space of time.

In our first year with our two children, Lorna and I decided not to travel 'home' for Christmas. The thought of packing toddler and baby equipment into the car filled us with dread, so we decided to stay in Dublin. 'Home' is a term used by culchies (people from outside Dublin who now live in Dublin) to say they are going to the place where they grew up. When people ask me where I'm from, I'll always say Laois. Laois is only sixty miles from Dublin and I've lived in Dublin longer than I've lived in Laois. My kids were born in Dublin, my house and job are in Dublin, as are most of my friends, but I'm still from Laois. 'I'm still Jenny from the block,' as in 'I'm still Bernard from the bog.'

This year, Lorna's parents were visiting us instead. It was Christmas Eve and we hadn't prepared any meals, so we decided to order a Chinese takeaway. I took the orders from my in-laws and Lorna asked me to get her a 3 in 1. However, when I asked the man in the takeaway on the phone for a 3 in 1, he told me he didn't know what that was. I proceeded to tell him.

Then came the impasse: 'No, we don't do that here.'

I then asked him if he could put chips, curry sauce and rice into a long silver tray. His reply: 'No, we don't do that.'

Now, I will admit I got a bit uppity and asked him if I could order a separate portion each of rice, chips and curry sauce. He replied, 'Yeah, if you want to do that.'

This really pissed me off and instead of just avoiding a row on Christmas Eve, I said, 'Well, I do want that, but I also want you to put them into one tray. It's called a three in one.'

He was now being argumentative. 'I've never heard of a three in one and I've been working here for over ten years.'

It was at this stage that I doubted myself. So, I called Lorna over. 'He's saying he's never heard of a three in one. They don't do it. They will only give them to us separately.'

'Jesus, Bernard, it's Christmas Eve, we're all hungry. Just

order it.' Now, I know Chinese cuisine is vast and unique and they certainly didn't invent or want anything to do with 3 in 1s – and I know 'curry' is Indian and it just basically means sauce – but I couldn't let it drop. Every Chinese takeaway in Ireland has served it.

Then it came, like a vocal dagger: 'You want the food or not?'

'Yes,' I snapped back. He told me it would be forty minutes, because they were busy. Yeah, I thought, busy preparing three separate portions of rice, chips and curry sauce, instead of putting it into one tray. I knew it was Christmas Eve. I knew it was a time for peace, but I called a Chinese friend of mine. His name is Leo. He used to do the door on the International Comedy Club and all the comics knew him. Like Liam Neeson in *Taken*, he had a particular set of skills. His skills were to point out to Irish people the idiotic things they thought about the Chinese. He had also worked for a brief time in Chinese restaurants in Dublin.

After what was quite a disappointing reaffirmation: 'Sorry, never heard of it' and 'Why are you calling me on Christmas Eve?' I felt I should apologise to the man who took my order. I waited the forty minutes and went out to the takeaway.

I always run through apologies in my head. I often visualise them as Hollywood moments. In this instance, I'm shattered, drenched in rain, standing in the doorway of the restaurant. He answers the door with the brown paper bag containing my order, looking all stern. I wipe the rain from my brow and exhale. 'I'm sorry, I know now that three in ones aren't real. I should never have doubted you.' He drops the bag and embraces me.

It didn't go down like this at all.

Imagine this Hollywood moment. I get to the top of the

stairs and there's a small lady behind the counter. I tell her my name and she goes looking through the dockets. 'No, we have no order for O'Shea.' I am livid. I explain all that has passed. The argument on the phone, the delay, the 3 in 1 debacle. She looks at me and says, 'We do three in ones.'

I'm ready to explode. I'm left with two options. Ring Lorna and tell her I've messed up or re-order the food. I re-order the food. She tells me it will be half an hour. I walk down the stairs and get into my car to wait. That prick, I think. Why did he tell me they didn't do 3 in 1s?

My phone rings. It's him again, the man from the takeaway. 'Your food is ready. We are waiting on you.'

'You just told me it would be another thirty minutes.'

'No, I didn't.'

'You didn't, but the old lady did.'

'What old lady? You want the food or not?'

'Okay, I'm coming back up.'

When I arrive at the top of the stairs, the old lady is sitting there and she says, 'It will be thirty minutes.'

'What? You just rang me and said it's ready. Well, not you, the man.'

'What man?'

'The man who said there's no three in ones.'

'I don't know that man.'

Then my phone rings again. It is him. Look, you're ringing me now, I thought. I answered the phone. 'I'm here and the old lady at your counter says it's not ready.'

'I'm standing at my counter now and I don't see you. You want the food or not? It's going cold.'

'Hold on.'

I put the old lady on the phone. She speaks to grumpy pants in Mandarin and then says, 'You are in the wrong restaurant.'

Okay, let me explain.

In the suburb where we live there are two identical buildings on the main street. And upstairs in the two buildings are two identically placed, but separate, Chinese restaurants. I rang one and ordered the food. Then went into the wrong one to pick up the food. Then re-ordered the same food in the wrong restaurant. I've seen less complicated Netflix docudramas. Also, I'd paid for both of them.

I go into the first restaurant and I'm in no mood to apologise. I just take my big, no, wait, *massive* brown bag of food and then sit with it in the other Chinese takeaway, waiting to collect another massive bag of food.

* * *

On my way home, I remembered that I had to get milk. I parked outside the supermarket. It was mobbed. The queues were nearly out the door as the shops wouldn't be open on Christmas Day. If any nation does panic buying for milk and bread, it's Ireland.

In a moment of olfactory stupidity, I put the two bags outside the car, because I didn't want them to stink it up while I was waiting in the queue in the supermarket. While queuing, I felt like doing a random survey asking, 'Have you ever heard of, or ordered, a three in one?' Fifteen minutes later, I headed back to the car, knowing the food must be freezing. Not at all. In fact, it was still pleasantly warm. It's what the four cats eating it must have thought. There I was in the car park of Tesco, holding milk and looking at nearly fifty euros' worth of Chinese takeaway being eaten by feral cats.

I put the milk on the roof of the car and pushed the cats off. Feral cats aren't like house cats. They fight back and they're very nasty. They'd destroyed the food. When I eventually got home, Lorna was not angry with me. Instead, she just calmly brought me into the downstairs toilet and told me how much she loved me and respected the difficult trauma I'd just been though. Oh, wait, she also told me I was completely f##king useless and that she and her family had waited so long for me they had decided to order a pizza. I should have told her it was her fault because she wanted a 3 in 1 but, hey, it's Christmas and the last thing I wanted was a fight.

'At least tell me you got the milk.'

'Yes, I got the milk.'

'Well, where is it?'

Now, I know I can be a difficult person to live with. I know that sometimes I bend the truth. But you have to believe me sometimes, even if that means I stare into your eyes and say, 'I was attacked by feral cats.'

That Christmas I slept on the couch.

PART THREE

An Eejit in the Family

18. He's fond of quoting his mum and dad, but he's hopeless at discipline.

If I'm ever asked what age I was when I first started stand-up comedy, I always say nineteen. My first ever gig was in Dundalk IT. My friend Danny, as part of our course, organised a comedy competition. I was the only one who entered. I won a crate of Harp lager and £50, which for a student was a lot of drinking money. However, my first gig was probably when I was six. It was Christmas time and me and my sister were allowed to stay up for *The Late Late Toy Show*. Just in case you're not Irish, *The Late Late Show* is Ireland's longest-running chat show. Unlike its UK or American counterparts, it swivels between all kinds of topics. In essence, the host can go from talking to neo-Nazi sympathisers to country and western singers to comedians, and Bono might be thrown in, along with a story about three Jack Russell terriers who've started a folk group. Once a year, there's a Christmas show. The host, with help from kids, reveals the toys that will be causing an increase in their parents' consumption of benzodiazepines that year.

It is Ireland's biggest TV event of the year, with a million plus viewers – one in every four people in the country. My kids are now allowed to stay up for it too, even though it starts at 9:30 p.m. and finishes at 11:30 p.m. In my day, being allowed to stay up for it was special. My bedtime, like that of most Irish kids of my ilk, was based around the nine o'clock news. In fact, there were two bedtimes: I had to be in bed before the news, but the cooler kids in the house, the rule-breakers, the rebels, the uncontrollables, were allowed to stay up until the weather was over at 9:20 p.m. But to be six and be allowed to stay up after the news until you fell asleep in a haze of diluted orange and tears due to the realisation that Santa was never going to bring you a full-scale electric car was monumental.

Nowadays, there is a genuine epidemic of poor sleep in children. Now that I'm a parent, getting our kids to sleep is akin to negotiating with terrorists. First, kids' TV doesn't start at 2 p.m. and finish at 6 p.m. any more. With Netflix, it's 24/7, so the negotiations start with a deal brokered according to TV time, in which I say, 'Olivia, you can have your programme, then it's Tadhg's, then we put our jammies on, then we go to bed.' I wish that our crepuscular adventures were that simple. There's another summit over who wants water, who goes up first, who gets their story first, who gets to be beside Daddy ... It goes on and on. I look back at the Northern Ireland peace process and think, 'It wasn't as hard as this.'

Eventually they fall asleep, but it doesn't end there. Within a few hours, they are in the bed with us, forever crunching our hips, shoving us into impossible sleeping positions and demanding all sorts of annoying and weird things at three in the morning. Tadhg went through a phase of demanding a ham wrap every night for a month. It's exhausting. The most bizarre part of it all is that I now can't sleep unless they come in to me. Even when we want sleep and have a clear run at a night with no children, myself and my wife wake at the appropriate times, like Pavlov's dogs.

Whereas my childhood bedtime was one of was strict regulation, now it's all about permissive persuasion. However, when the opportunity struck to criticise my parents' regime during the ads for the *Toy Show*, I took it. My first-ever comedy routine, when I was six, was 'Mammy and Daddy's Top Five Sayings'. I jumped down off the kitchen table and in front of my mother, father, three sisters and granny declared, 'at number five, it's Daddy with … "You're very near it now."' My father would always say that as a warning, to which, as I got a little bit older and braver, I would reply, 'How near?' and mimic the distance with my thumb and index finger. 'This near? Or this near?' This only drove him more demented. However, his threat was real. He had every intention of carrying it out. At the tender age of four, Olivia now knows that I will NEVER carry out my threats. I said to her once, 'That's it, no dancing class this weekend – you're too bold.'

She cried and then stopped and told me, 'Daddy, if you don't bring me to dancing, then you and Tadhg won't be able to go for your nice breakfast and you'll have to stay here.' Well, *touché*, four-year-old girl, *touché*. I'm pretty sure if we ever even threatened to give Olivia a smack on the bottom, she would get in touch with Amnesty International and several media outlets. She knows I'm weak and she gets what she wants most of the time, but that's okay, because she's my little girl and she is never leaving home, ever, and she will cuddle me for ever and tell me that I'm amazing and strong. She will also never be allowed to have a boyfriend.

Looking at my father to see how he reacted to my first gag, I moved swiftly on. 'At number four, it's Mammy with "I can't have anything nice with ye in this house."' I always thought, when she said this, 'What do we have in this house that's nice?' It was the eighties – only rich people had nice things. However, her constant efforts to have anything nice, even in the good room, would eventually be broken. If you're reading this, Mum, I will admit I broke the following things. The Waterford Crystal vase. The Belleek pottery clock. The Wedgwood porcelain figure of a woman in a pink dress given to you by a great aunt, which, I later found out on the internet, was actually really expensive. I'm sorry I broke her, pretending she was an action figure. Oh, and every single hairdryer you ever bought for yourself and the silver picture frame in the sitting room.

I even say, 'I can't have anything nice in the house' to my kids now. It's like they have an evil twin inside them when Mammy or Daddy gets anything nice. They want our phones, our dinners, even our shoes. In fact, I'll say it now: 'I can't have anything nice in my house any more.' Take the very expensive Italian biscotti that a friend gave me. I foolishly left them on the table and within two minutes the kids had destroyed them. To add insult to injury, they didn't even eat them. Tadhg exclaimed, while standing on the remains, 'I don't like these, Daddy.'

Back to my family home and I'd only three to go and the *Toy Show* could be back any second, so with a slightly flagging audience, I shouted out number three. 'At number three it's Mammy again, with "If your friends jumped off a cliff, would you jump off a cliff?"' When I got older, I used to reply, 'We live in the midlands, Mammy, there are no cliffs.' I thought I was hilarious, but she would she always retort with, 'It's a pity you weren't so smart in school.'

Mothers always have the ability to cut you down to size, no matter how good or 'clever' your cheekiness gets. You can say anything and she will just take the main word of your sentence and give it back to you. Example: 'Tidy up your room, Bernard, it's a mess.' I would normally say, 'It's a mess because everything I have is crap'. To which she would reply, 'I'll give you crap, if you don't go in and tidy it up.' It made absolutely no sense whatsoever. Mothers apply it to everything. 'Ma, give me money for my lunch.' The reply? 'I'll give you money for your lunch alright, you will be given sandwiches.'

The crowd were now warming up and I was at number two. 'At number two, it's Daddy with "Close that f##king door."' This was due, in most part, to 'not letting the heat out' but also because children, even your own, are really annoying and he wanted us to leave him in peace. My father didn't generally have to deal with us. When he wanted to watch the news, we all had to be quiet. This was true of most fathers in the seventies and eighties. If I tried this now at home – told Lorna and the kids to not move a muscle while I watched something – they would laugh at me. Not in a metaphorical way, but in an actual, real way - they *would* laugh at me. Now, if there is a family event on in our house, anybody who wants to watch a match is relegated to a smaller TV in the front room. This is why men have sheds. It's a stereotype, I know, but there is truth to it. Instead of a loud roar to tell all in the house to be quiet, instead we can take ourselves truly away from it all and go to sea on a stationary, land-locked spruce ship, with Wi-Fi. I have always been intensely snobbish and openly scornful of 'man caves' or 'man sheds', but now I crave one. Alas, we have no space left in my home, as our three-bed semi-d is doing the job it was actually built for – giving us somewhere to live. Our garden is tiny, though, no room for a shed there. Our attic is too small and I've been told if it's ever converted to a room, it will be a bedroom. The irony of it all was that I had the perfect 'man cave' when I desperately didn't need it: my tiny bedsit in the inner city, which I rented for four years in my twenties. It was minute, yet everyone I knew stayed in it because it was so central.

This didn't mean that I wasn't a laughing stock among my friends. I was the guy who lived in a box. Yet its design is exactly what my wife now consumes in her dreams. She is constantly looking at US programmes about the Tiny House revolution and it's her dream to live in one. The bedsit, or 'studio apartment' if you're posh, is just that. My own tiny home had a shower, a sink, a cooker, a fridge, a chair and a TV, all in the same room. In the 'bedroom' there was just enough space for a bed. I had practically no clothes or belongings except my guitar. I was also penniless. Thus, because of my own dire financial situation, while I pursued a career in comedy, I was years ahead of architectural design and the vogue today for 'minimal' living. I do, however, remember thinking that it was like living in a prison cell, except I didn't really have enough money to eat three times a day and I got no exercise at all. I never had to say 'Close that f##king door', though, because there were none.

Before I get to the number one saying from my mother and father, I have to preface this by describing the unique relationship between a son and his mother. Mothers love their daughters, but they really love their sons. You can see it in their eyes when they give birth. They are thinking, 'I've just given birth to the man I've always wanted to marry.' There is nothing a son can do to deflect the intensity of a mother's gaze. When it comes to a mother–daughter relationship, mothers expect maturity from their daughters and basic co-operation by the age of three, whereas with their sons, most Irish mothers still worry if their little boy is getting enough to eat well into his sixties. So the day when a boy tells his mother to 'f##k off' is tragic, yet unavoidable. I remember saying it.

My mother snapped, 'Did you just tell your mother to f##k off?'

Instantly I tried to redact it. 'No, I said feck off.'

'No, you didn't. I heard you say it.' And then it comes. It flows out of every mammy's mouth, like an AK-47 riddling you with guilt bullets: 'AND ALL I DO FOR YOU'. It's one of those sayings you have no come-back from – it's a killer. Parents do everything for their children and they're never going to get back what they sacrificed, ever. You just get to watch your own children someday turn around to you and tell you to 'f##k off' and then you can continue the ancient oral tradition of saying to them, 'And all I do for you.'

> The children now love luxury; they have bad manners, contempt for authority; they show disrespect for elders and love chatter in place of exercise. Children are now tyrants, not the servants of their households. They no longer rise when elders enter the room. They contradict their parents, chatter before company, gobble up dainties at the table, cross their legs, and tyrannise their teachers.

Socrates said that in 335 BC. It will happen. I'm not happy about it, I'm just prepared for it.

19. He hasn't a clue how to deliver a baby, but that didn't stop him giving the midwife instructions.

I've sat for hours trying to think of a word that sums up excitement and fear. Think about it: there should be one. The closest I've come is 'trepidation', but it doesn't work – it's too close to fear. 'Hope' is too flimsy and too positive, so I've come up with a new word: 'fearcitement'. This word, for me, explains the feeling we had prior to our first child being born. Every time Lorna moved in the bed throughout her pregnancy, I thought, 'It's happening', followed by her telling me to calm down. We were petrified.

Lorna was adamant she wanted a natural birth and was always confused by other women who would laugh it off. 'You'll be screaming for the drugs' was the consistent reply. Little did I know that when we did eventually get in the car to go to the hospital, I was the one who'd need the drugs. Every moan I thought was a sign that the baby was on its way. Lorna eventually shouted at me in the car on the way to the hospital, 'If you don't calm down, you're not coming in with me.'

First thing to note for soon-to-be first-time dads, whatever a woman in labour says, agree with it, or do it. Second, maternity hospitals are warm. By the time we got our bed in the ward, I was nearly down to my underpants. Third, don't moan to heavily pregnant women about how warm you're feeling.

I thought that when we got into the hospital, we would be having the baby within a few minutes. Two days later, no baby. Lorna kept saying, 'Did you not learn anything from the pre-baby course?' No, I didn't. I mostly kept looking at the plastic baby model and wondering was it like those baby dolls that wee themselves, which I buy for my nieces for Christmas. When we were eventually brought up to the labour ward (which I thought we were already on) the action started. You instantly become an expert on a hormone called oxytocin, the love drug, and on breathing.

At first, my wife was happy I was there. She laughed when I asked if I could take some oxytocin home for round two (a risky joke in a labour ward, but it worked) but within a few hours she had turned on me. 'Bernard, you don't know how to deliver a baby. Shut the f##k up, you're embarrassing me.' This because I told the midwife that I was an expert in delivering babies, because I'd once delivered a lamb on live telly and I presumed this would be the same. The midwife told me very clearly that it wasn't, but I thought it was, so we'll agree to disagree. It was around the fifth or sixth time that I told my wife to 'breathe through the pain, honey' that she asked me to leave. I told her again that she would release oxytocin soon and she'd want me there. It seemed like every time I tried to do what I thought was right instead of doing what she actually asked me to do, it upset her. Eventually, as on the birth of all our children, I fell asleep on one of the big blue sponge mats provided for a floor birth, beside the bed. It's the heat that makes me sleepy – I do the same in the cinema.

When I woke up, Lorna was in a lot of pain. She squeezed my hand so tightly every time she had a contraction, I kind of felt she was trying to hurt me. I was going to bring this up with her, but I thought, this time maybe not. Eventually, our first child, Olivia, was born. When the nurses held her up and gave her to Lorna, it was truly a magical moment. A moment where you will always say and do the right thing. I looked at my wife and said, 'Well done.' This heartfelt comment was to ruin my life for the following few weeks.

Even though she had just given birth to our first child, she stared me down and reiterated, '*Well done*? Are you serious, Bernard? After all this labour, I give birth and the first thing you say to me is "well done". Is there anything else you'd like to contribute?'

I thought about it. I could say sorry now and tell her I love her … or I could make the situation lighter by cracking a joke that would put everybody at ease. I went with the latter. 'Look at the big red head on her, she's mine anyway.' At this stage, the nurses were trying to make polite conversation and leave.

Lorna looked at me. 'Bernard, get me water.' Thank God, a job. There is nothing better to get you out of an awkward situation than somebody asking you to get them something.

Over the next few days, I did lots of jobs. Lorna still recounts the seven hours it took me to find a breast pump. 'The nurses in the hospital told me that you could rent the pump from a provider on the same street as the hospital. Bernard found the exact same pump and price except forty miles away in Wicklow. I've never known someone to make the most simple things the most difficult, and the most difficult things the simplest.'

We decided to baptise Olivia. Neither myself nor my wife are devout Catholics, but I joked constantly that it would improve her chances of getting into heaven, thus probably being able to put in a good word for me, to get me out of purgatory. I like the idea of our children having the same experiences as me: communion, confirmation and going to weddings and funerals are, for the most part, good fun. I do, however, have a bit of a problem with confession. Telling a six- or seven-year-old child to make up a lie to tell a man who is going to forgive that lie anyway just doesn't sit right with me. When Olivia asked me, at a family wedding, what those tiny rooms were in the corner of the church, I had to explain confession to her. 'So, if I hit Tadhg and told God and the priest I did, then it goes away?' I tried to be more nuanced and started to tell her that religion is a belief system and that when we do wrong things, regardless of who we tell, there are consequences. I was about fifteen seconds in when she said, 'Are they magic boxes, Daddy?'

'Yes,' I replied, 'they are magic boxes.' Over to you, national school, I'm done trying to explain.

Olivia suffered from first-child syndrome. Her baptism was attended by nearly a hundred people. For her first birthday, we got the house painted and invited everyone we knew. Anything she touched was sterilised. Her clothes, my God, her clothes. With grandparents and family buying her new outfits every week, Lorna joked, then seriously commented, that we could open a baby boutique. It's a far cry from Tadhg, who could be carrying a box of broken glass while sipping on diesel and we would just think, 'He'll be fine'. As for Seán, our third, God help him. By the time he becomes a toddler, he'll either be tied up under the stairs by his siblings or holding down a part-time job. That's how it works. Now that Olivia and Tadhg are walking, talking little people it makes it easier, but even so, when Seán came along, Lorna and I looked at each other one day, when she was covered in puke and the kids were playing on my guitar case. I said to her, 'We were just out of the woods and now it's like we have to start all over again.' To which Tadhg replied, 'Are we gown to da wood?'

Olivia, who grew up in the transience of the city centre, consistently watching *Peppa Pig*, talks in a posh accent. 'Dod, are we going to the playground todoy?' Meanwhile, Tadhg has grown up in Blanchardstown and says things in a broad Dublin accent, like, 'I wanna go see da lionzz', and 'I wanna yog-art.' Olivia tells him, 'Yoghurt, Tadhg, it is called a yoghurt.'

Going from one to two children is like going from owning a dog to running a zoo, and going from two to three feels like we're on a safari, where the animals can attack us at any time. Having a girl helps. It may be stereotypical, but it's true. They mature quicker and are smart. As the old saying goes, girls will wreck your head, boys will wreck your house. Young boys (and I was one myself) are a bit stupid. Whereas Olivia always wanted to pick out her own clothes and, when inclined, can dress herself, Tadhg is a different story. I once saw him actually head-butt a T-shirt, thinking that this was how he would get it on him. He's easier to deal with, however. He forgets things. Women never forget. A few weeks ago, I brought the two of them to the zoo. Before we even got to the entrance, Olivia started: 'Dod, can we get chocolate? Because you said at Christmas [three months earlier] that the next time you brought me to the zoo, I could get chocolate on the way in and a Minions ice-cream on the way out and Granny O'Shea gave you ten euros to buy me a magazine as well, so you can spend that on getting me the ice-cream instead …

okay?' Meanwhile, Tadhg is pointing at a crow: 'Luke, Daddy, lionzz.' But they are generally exceptionally well-behaved children – all you have to do is give them exactly what they want at precisely the right time and things go generally okay.

Olivia will also say frequently when they're with me, 'Dad, me and Tadhg have decided we want to go to a restaurant.' Now, I'm not a pushover, but if there is one nearby that's reasonably priced, why not? When I was growing up, however, I could count on one finger how many times we went to a restaurant. We would go to the same one in Limerick city every year on our way to my dad's home. I would run into the restaurant and try to order things like hake or crème caramel, but my father or mother would always say, 'You won't eat it. You can order off the kiddies' menu.' I was determined not to let that happen to my kids, but when Olivia wanted 'muscles' because she thought they were like the muscles on *Supergirl*, I quickly turned into my father and told her, 'You won't eat it,' which was followed by a barrage of tears until I let her get them. When she saw them, she said, 'Yuck, disgusting … you have them, Daddy.'

Tadhg looked at them and told me, 'They luke loike slugs'. But the trend here is obvious. Since the birth of our third child, I'm now the actual father of two. Before Seán was born, they went to Mammy for everything: sleep, comfort, reassurance. Now I'm their comfort blanket. They sleep with me, roar at me and laugh at me. I'm generally their dogsbody. Lorna is loving it, constantly reminding me that it was she who went through years of no sleep. Now it's payback time, I suppose, but I don't mind it. I no longer say things like 'I'll babysit', when Lorna would again remind me, '*They're your children. You don't babysit your own children.*'

I knew what parenting was all about before I had children. I was brilliant at looking at other parents and pointing out exactly what they were doing wrong. My sisters took great glee in constantly reminding me, 'Wait and see, Bernard.' Simply put, I knew how to raise children when I had no children. Now, I'm close to useless, but in a fun way. According to Olivia, 'Telling us what to do isn't good for you, Dad,' and it isn't.

Everybody keeps telling you that your life will change when you have children. We were being polite when we listened, but deep down, we thought nothing would. Christ, we were wrong. First, we were living in a flat with a balcony. When Olivia started to crawl, we knew we had to find a house. I had also started a new job. Why is it that you have to make all the most important life decisions in the space of three to six weeks? Every young family has the same story – it's almost like it's planned by banks to make sure you are stressed up to your eyeballs in your mid-thirties, young enough to take the stress, but not old enough to die from it.

The travel system, finding a crèche, the bottles and nappies ... When you look at modern parenting, you have to ask yourself, why? Why do we knowingly put ourselves though this? Everybody tells you parenting is hard, but no one ever writes or says the truth, which is this: ninety per cent of the time you just don't want to do it. For instance, washing Tadhg is a horrific nightmare of tears and bubbles that make me want to run away to another country, so my wife does it. When she's not there and I have to do it, she warns me, 'Bernard, you have to bathe them or they'll be smelly. Do you want them to be the smelly kids?' But when I say 'bath time', Tadhg screams so much and Olivia puts on her swimming goggles, and that sends signals to my brain so strong that I end up giving them chocolate and telling them, 'If Mammy asks if I washed you, you say yes, okay?' I then try my best to make it look like I've washed them by using wipes. Lorna loses the rag over this type of behaviour.

I used to come up with thousands of excuses for my lack of effort as a parent. 'Bernard, did you clean the bedlinen?'

'No, I was trying to, honey, but Seán had a cough so bad that I had to hold him for six hours.'

Or, 'Bernard, did you cut Tadhg's nails?'

'No, I was going to, but the dishwasher was broken and I spent the last five hours fixing it.'

Eventually, I broke. One day, when Lorna returned from town, Tadhg met her at the door and said, 'Daddy gave us chocolate if we said we'd had a bath.' Before Lorna had the chance to give out to me again, I spoke the truth. In a scene that resembled Russell Crowe's speech in *Gladiator* I stood up for truth and exclaimed to the world and my wife, 'I didn't wash them, or do the beds, or cook them dinner, or make them play outside, or do anything they didn't want to do because … I DON'T WANT TO.'

It's hard to argue with someone who says, 'I don't want to.' I should know this because it's what toddlers say all the time and we have a few of them at home. Needless to say, my 'I don't want to' speech didn't go down too well. It actually made me do more around the house and with the kids because I felt guilty for being honest and blurting out the truth about the elixir of happiness: just doing nothing.

My fortieth birthday was on the horizon recently and my wife asked me, 'Instead of doing nothing, what do you want for your fortieth?' I told her I wanted us to go away together somewhere nice for a night. She didn't want to as she felt Seán was too young and she didn't want to be away from him. We eventually found a babysitting solution and booked a night away in a hotel not too far away from the house, about an hour and a half's drive.

When we got there, my wife had a few spa treatments lined up and I watched an entire football match on my own, for the first time in six years. I did notice that it was a dreadful game, but just being able to do it was enough. We hadn't had a meal together in years, so we ordered room service and watched *Grand Designs* while I broke the Nespresso machine. We were in bed asleep at 7:30. That's what both of us crave: sleep.

When I think back to the days of just doing stand-up and getting up at midday, I never realised that I led such a privileged life. I read once that the KGB used sleep deprivation to get the truth out of its agents and also to torture enemies. Never did I realise our three children were working for them. Most people would think, first night out, get drunk; but no, sleep is the new cocaine. However, even in the hotel, I was awake at 2:30 a.m. Why? Because Tadhg comes into me at that time, demanding food and water and dinosaurs. Lorna was awake at 3:30 a.m. Why? Because Seán wakes at that time for his bottle. And we were both awake at 6:30, because that's the time Olivia demands that the whole house gets up to watch *Frozen*.

There we were, awake, not able to do the one thing we wanted to do. Except there was one thing we *could* do. I started to become amorous and was eventually stopped. 'No, Bernard.'

'But we can't sleep and we're in a lovely hotel room. I know you don't have a headache and it's not your special woman time, so, why not?'

She kissed me on the lips, pushed me down onto the bed, like she was re-enacting a scene from a Mills and Boon novel, and whispered into my ear, 'Because I don't want to.'

20. He made a total fool of himself in the supermarket and didn't even know why.

When I was single, going grocery shopping was just a chore. In fact, I disliked it so much that I managed to avoid it for nearly two years. Before I had a family or a full-time job, most of my work was doing stand-up comedy gigs. If you can get enough work, being a comedian is a ridiculously pleasurable existence. I would work Thursday, Friday and Saturday nights; the rest of the week, month, year, was free time. In fact, I can honestly swear that I didn't even know when it was a bank holiday, or a Tuesday for that matter.

I would wake up around noon and my first meal of the day would be lunch. I might then go for a walk, then get some dinner and, most nights, a takeaway. My hunter-gatherer path would have resembled a scrawly etching of cafés, carveries and Chinese takeaways. What was the point in cooking? I was throwing out nearly everything I bought, so I just stopped. Dublin is an expensive place to eat out in, but I had it down to around €150 a week for three meals a day. One small caveat, though. I couldn't afford to buy a car, clothes or alcohol. Yes, alcohol. I gave up my most prized obsession with which I'd had an intense affair, culminating in that New Year's sleep in a bush outside a petrol station. But I never thought that five years later, going shopping would be the highlight of my week.

I have a gem in my lazy locker. Lorna hates shopping much more than I do. So, when asked about housework, I can always pipe up and say proudly, 'Yeah, but I do all the shopping.' In the last few years, I've grown to love it. I actually got properly excited recently when one of our local supermarkets changed its layout. I know where most of everything is in that shop, but I had to go explore it all over again. It was like those Hollywood movies where the geeky girl takes off her glasses and fluffs out her hair and reveals how sexy she can be with a few tweaks. Yep, that's how weird simple grocery shopping has gotten for me. I even know off by heart what coin – €1 or €2 – each supermarket takes in its trolleys.

Why has shopping become club night for me? Simple: kids. I'll be honest, you need a break when your house is full of them. My wife knows at this stage that I'll burst out through the windows to go and get toilet paper rather than go through the combat training that is trying to clean Tadhg. Also, as Olivia has got older, I've become more confident going places with her on my own. She would always say to me, when I'd grab my keys off the table, 'Are you going to the shop now, Daddy?'

On one wet and grey Saturday morning, I replied, 'I am; would you like to come with me?'

After Olivia screaming '*Yes*' several times, Lorna got us ready. Yes, *us*. She made me pack Olivia a bag, which I thought was ridiculous – we were only going to the shop. Oh, how wrong I was. She put on Olivia's pink raincoat and hat and told me sternly, 'Don't take your eyes off her for one second.'

'Christ, Lorna, we're going to the shops, we're not crossing a war zone – have some confidence in me.' In hindsight she shouldn't have had confidence in me.

I strapped Olivia into her car seat. We beeped and waved Mum and Tadhg goodbye and made the perilous 1.3-kilometre journey to the supermarket. Now, Olivia tends to ask me questions that bring my innermost fears into reality. It's almost like she has a secret power that enables her to read my mind. She said, 'Do you know what to do with me when we get there, Daddy?'

I instantly replied, 'Yeah, of course,' but I didn't. I didn't have one iota. All I know is that I got angry, really angry when the parent and baby parking spots were all taken up. Now I know why they are where they are. Proximity is everything when chauffeuring the toddler classes. It was a real test of physical power and cognitive ability to carry Olivia and our bags to the trolley bay. Before I put her on the ground, I warned her. 'Olivia, you do not run away now, hold on to Daddy.' I got the trolley and easily put her in it. Simple. I didn't know what Lorna was harping on about. Olivia's little legs were at full stretch, but she was loving being in the trolley with Daddy, and then she said, 'This is much more fun with you, Daddy.'

As we approached the door, I could see two ladies pointing and smiling at us as we entered the shop. I thought to myself, 'I am a good – no, wait – a *great* father, and do you know what? This comes naturally to me.' Olivia was enjoying it so much, she actually roared, 'Wah hoo!' as we rolled along to the cheese counter.

It was then that a man approached me. 'Are you okay there?'

Confused, Olivia and I both looked at him. 'Yeah, thank you,' I said and we pushed off. As we approached the frozen-food section, a staff member asked me if I would like a hand with my daughter. 'I'm okay, thanks.' At this stage, this thirty-seven-year-old man and two-and-a-half-year-old girl were both utterly confused as to why we were being asked if we needed help. We were having possibly the best daddy–daughter shopping day ever. So far, everybody was smiling, some even laughing, at us. We were acing this retail experience.

Then we got to the checkout. It was then that I realised I had made an error. A pretty dangerous, embarrassing error. When I saw all the other parents with their children, I realised I'd put Olivia the wrong way around in the trolley, so that she was facing the front. No wonder she was having the time of her life. She was basically in the toddler version of a Ferrari. It all became clear.

I said, 'Olivia, get up, we have to face the other way.' Now what would you imagine her reply was?

A: Of course, Daddy. This is an extremely dangerous way to put a toddler in a metal cage, because if I fell forward, I would seriously hurt myself.
B: No, you've embarrassed yourself in front of everybody now, so I'll just stay in this position.
C: NO, NO, NO, NO, NO, NO, NO, I DON'T WANT TO. NO, NO, NO, NO, DADDY. NO, NO, NO.

It was A. No, it was C.

The worst was yet to come. As we got to the checkout, the assistant tried his best to coax Olivia out. This just made it worse. Not because he wasn't being kind – but you should never corner a wild animal or a toddler: it's as bad as saying 'You're tired.' The whole shop was looking at us. It's at these times in your life you wonder if they actually bus people in to see you in your weakest moments. I think there were about ten to fifteen thousand people at one stage, watching and judging us. Even a wise old couple, who had the air of having seen this a thousand times, couldn't calm her down. I never thought I'd be that parent. For years, I'd see kids have complete meltdowns in shopping centres and I would blame the parents. Now I was that parent.

I had to react. I did the one thing that I knew would work. I gave her a bar of chocolate. If you are one of those people who thinks they will never give their children chocolate or, worse, you tell people you don't … f##k off, just f##k off, you are deluded or lying. Chocolate is brilliant. Chocolate fixes problems. Chocolate is God. Chocolate is a portable vacuum for tears. Without chocolate, Calpol SixPlus and baby wipes, modern parenting doesn't happen. And, if you are one of those liars who tells people, 'I don't give my child chocolate,' guess what? Granny and Granddad do.

As she ate her way through the chocolatey arse of a hippopotamus, a surge of guilt began to burst out from my brain and flood my heart. Guilt, the worst of all feelings. Yes, she wasn't crying, but was I poisoning her? Could I not just listen to her scream for half an hour? Had I given her a terrible habit that would result in her being a drug addict and would she think it all started because Daddy put her in a trolley the wrong way around on a wet Saturday morning in suburban west Dublin? No. No, it won't. I've decided that unless I've intentionally hurt someone, physically or otherwise, I'm not entertaining guilt any more. I should have just let her sit forward-facing. So what? That's how I would have liked to sit. In her own words, 'I can see more this way, Daddy.'

21. He spoiled my dream of a perfect family holiday just like the ones I'd had as a child.

When I was growing up, holidays were non-existent. It wasn't from lack of effort, it was just lack of money. There were four of us kids, it was the eighties and anybody who had ever held a fifty-pound note in Ireland at that time was deemed a celebrity. Even though my mum had been born and raised in my home town of Durrow, my dad was from Kerry, from a village called Annascaul. Our 'holiday' was to go up and down, on the one day, to visit our uncle, auntie and great auntie. That is, a hundred and sixty miles each way. This was in a country that had no motorways and a traffic jam in every town en route. It would take over three and a half hours each way, seven hours in total, just in the car. My father loved his cars, possibly a trait he passed on to me. ('You love your car more than us' – my wife, circa 2017.) He had a yellow Toyota Celica for most of the eighties. He loved it. I can see why – it was an affordable sports car with a big engine. Take a moment for thought here, though. There were four kids, my mother and my granny living in the house as well. Including himself, that would be seven.

My father bought a sports car that had to transport seven people. We still find it hilarious today but, hey, a nice car is a nice car.

My mother would sit in the front. The youngest girl, Cáit, would sit on her lap. My granny, who smoked, would sit in the middle seat, not beside the window, because my mother wouldn't let us roll down the windows in case we all got earaches and died. My two other sisters would sit either side of Granny and I would go in the boot. When I think of the NASA-style instruction and expense we go to with our children and their child seats – forward-facing, rear-facing, to Isofix (the elaborate base into which you click your baby's car seat) or not to Isofix, that is the question – whereas I would travel seven hours, over three hundred miles, from five years of age, in the boot of a sports car. I didn't have Isofix: I had hope and the Our Father. The car didn't even have rear seatbelts – at the time, they were an optional extra.

What really did my head in, though, apart from twisty bends, was the palaver our parents would put us through before we took off on our journey. I'm pretty sure every child of the eighties has heard this: 'Go now, because we're not stopping.' You could be screaming in agony. Your kidneys could be actually bursting. You could pass a town the Irish translation of which could be 'the small land of a thousand toilets', but Dad would not stop. 'I told you to go back at the house, because we're not stopping.'

As I said before, when Olivia was fussing over mussels, the biggest treat for us at the time was to eat out. Prior to the Celtic Tiger, eating in a restaurant was only for our erstwhile Taoiseach, Charlie Haughey, or tourists. So, even though I wouldn't be allowed to choose, having to settle for sausage and chips, if we were on track time-wise (God forbid one of my sisters wanted to have the luxury of urinating along the way), I'd get jelly and ice cream.

However, my wife had a completely different upbringing, especially when it came to car journeys. They were stoppers. They would stop in the shop, stop to look at scenery, even stop for rests – oh, the luxury. I am not a stopper. When we first started going out, I didn't drive, so I didn't care how we got there. However, now that I do, she drives me insane on journeys. We will be all in the car with the kids and Lorna will say, 'Can you stop in the shop? I've to get a Diet Coke and a magazine.' This drives me bonkers. Why? Because you had all the time before we took off to pop to the shop and get your Diet Coke, I'd think. Once, driving to Kerry, I told her, 'If I hear Diet Coke once more, you can walk.'

I have offered solutions. I made a Lorna travel kit. It is a plastic bag with a Diet Coke and a magazine in it. She declined, saying the Coke was too warm and that she liked to pick out the magazine. We now take separate cars when we can.

However, without her in my life, I probably would never have gone on a proper holiday.

* * *

When I was in college, every summer was spent working. When I finished college, I was completely penniless. I went away for a lot of weekends abroad to football matches and with friends and have seen some of the world as a working comic, but spending two weeks doing nothing, only being on a holiday, was alien to me until I met my wife. We were together about a year and a half when she told me about this weird phenomenon. We decided to go to Italy, which you will recall, dear reader, from the 'balls in the swimming pool' story.

He spoiled my dream of a perfect family holiday just like the ones I'd had as a child.

Italy is a beautiful country. The food, people and cities are just majestic, but, Christ almighty, their public transport is diabolical and that, coming from an Irishman, is not good. I can see why they love their cars, because their train staff are always on strike. I've never been to Italy when there wasn't a train or bus strike. Why do they even have public transport? What do their train drivers do?

We couldn't get to any of our chosen destinations because, probably due to their public transport problems, like in Ireland, they drive everywhere and the roads were choked with traffic. We eventually reached our hotel in a town on Lake Garda called Riva del Garda, through a combination of sleigh, hope and taxis. Being on a lake, the only way to get to the other towns was by boat, but guess what? The boats were on strike, too. Being stuck beside a lake for two weeks together resulted in an engagement ring being thrown at me, but let's begin at the beginning.

The hotel we were staying in was fine, clean and bright. We were on a tight budget but the town wasn't. Riva is expensive. We didn't know this. But then again, like most of our disastrous holidays, we always end up in a town, city or on an island that is relatively cheap to get to, but where you'd need a small mortgage to buy a Cornetto. A middle-aged couple who offered local walking tours of Lake Garda from the hotel eventually offered to take us on a little hike up the old road of Garda that was not used by cars. It was now used by mountain bikers and extreme-sport enthusiasts. It was halfway up this mountain road that I found out that my wife was afraid of heights. A sharp tug at my shirt told me she wanted to head back to the town, but she suggested I go on.

I told her not to be stupid: I'd head back with her. Then our conversation turned quickly into a to and fro of 'No, I'll go back with you', 'No, you go on' until it escalated into a full-on row.

'Is everything okay?' shouted the woman.

'Yes, fine,' my wife shouted back.

'What is wrong with you, Lorna?' I was genuinely worried.

'I'm afraid of heights, okay? I want to go back.'

Now, instead of just leaving it alone and comforting her and letting her head back down the road, I did what I do best and made the situation a thousand times worse by trying to convince her she had nothing to be afraid of.

'No, Bernard, I don't need you to help me, I just want you to go on ahead with them and I'll see you back in the hotel.'

'Don't be silly, Lorna. We're not even that high and there's a road underneath us.' It went on like this until the couple walked back down to us. I told them, 'Lorna is afraid of heights, so we're going back.'

The lady turned to Lorna and said, 'It's okay. I used to suffer from your illness.'

Ha! 'Your *illness*!' I started roaring laughing. 'Your illness,' I repeated. Then I looked up and an engagement ring was heading towards my retina.

'You stupid dick. I was fine with heading home, but you had to make a show of me in front of these strangers,' and she stormed off. What seemed like a lifetime but was probably only thirty seconds later, I was left with two complete strangers, one of them holding an engagement ring, right on the side of a cliff in northern Italy. The woman kept talking about Lorna's 'illness', but I didn't find it funny any more. I left them and walked after her. A lot of grovelling later and the engagement was back on. The lesson here is, if somebody is afraid of heights, let them go back: don't make them climb a steep mountain.

However, my wife was to learn all about my hidden fear on our first family holiday five years later.

Lorna has idyllic memories of holidaying in a caravan, going around Ireland with her family. When she first suggested to me that we should go on a caravan holiday, my reply was that I would stay in the caravan that had a reception, swimming pool and room service and she could stay in the caravan with none of those things. She would not believe me when I said, 'I hate caravans.' She started telling me that they were actually very nice nowadays and that my feelings towards them were unfounded. I reminded her of her 'illness' and told her, 'You don't like heights; I don't like caravans.'

The thing is, my wife is petite. She is four foot four and a half. She always states that the 'half' is really important, like a toddler telling you, 'I'm not four, I'm four and a half.' I, on the other hand, am six foot two and suffer from claustrophobia. I can't breathe in small spaces, and the thought of sleeping in them makes me extremely anxious. Caravans to me are just tiny, uncomfortable houses that are designed for me to hit my head off them in various places, not to mention impaling myself on hidden drawer handles.

Lorna kept harping on about how Olivia would love it. Kids do love caravans. That is because they're like tiny Wendy houses with real things in them. Like those play cookers, except that in a caravan they are dangerous. However, enough badgering took place between winter and spring – or September to May, because we don't get seasons in Ireland, just the 'odd good day' – that we decided, when Olivia was two, that we'd take her on a magical caravan holiday. My father-in-law drove the caravan to a beautiful caravan park on the west coast of Clare. He did this because if you've never driven before, towing a caravan can be very dangerous. This I did not care about. I cared more about all the people behind us, trying to get on with their lives, stuck behind a f##king caravan.

Lorna was convinced that I'd love it. I wanted to love it, even though I banged my head off the door the very first time I stepped into it. It was tiny enough as it was, but we were still in the throes of the 'newly born' phase with Olivia, so we'd brought most of Mothercare's stock, and by the time we'd finished unpacking, there was even less room.

However, when I did step out of the caravan and looked across the wild Atlantic Clare coast, it was absolutely stunning. We do sometimes forget how beautiful Ireland can be, especially when the weather is good. I looked out to sea and the boats were making their way to the Aran Islands. The sun bounced up and down off the Atlantic, like butter being spread on hot toast. The waves pounded against the little pier at Doolin and the sound of the seabirds mixed gently with the deep hush of the sea. It was gorgeous.

And then it pissed rain. Those few seconds were the best it was to get. It rained so hard that night that Olivia asked me, 'Are we on a boat, Daddy?'

The thing about being over six foot tall and trying to sleep in a caravan is that your feet are in the kitchen at all times. Every time I turned over, I opened the fridge. When I did eventually get some sleep, my left foot accidentally made an Italian meringue. I woke up feeling exhausted, while my four-foot-four-and-a-half wife and two-year-old were exploding with energy, ready to explore our new surroundings. However, unlike in films where it's always dry and bright the next morning, Ireland doesn't do that. It was raining again. In fact, it hadn't stopped. It had also turned windy, so windy that when it did stop raining, the wind blew sea water in off the shore and it lashed against the van. I swear if you listened closely enough, you could hear sharks talking to each other: 'Turn around, it's too dangerous,' and 'I'm not attacking anybody unless they're wearing a jumper – it's too cold here.' It was freezing. It would have been perfect for thirty-something singles making mad passionate love all day only to break for an espresso, sipping it while gazing at the ocean, naked from the waist down; but with a two-year-old who has abundant energy, it's hell.

Breakfast outside would possibly have resulted in death, so we had our cereal and contemplated what to do. My wife had picked up a brochure for a leisure centre, which had an aquarium, in Lahinch, so we decided to go. Our first mistake was to tell Olivia we were going to see the fish. Advice: never tell a toddler where you're going or what you're doing until you get there. The second-best piece of parenting advice I heard is that you should treat toddlers like tiny, drunk people. It's so true. When they act up, it reminds me of when I used to work in bars. I say the exact same thing to my toddlers today as I did to drunks years ago: 'That's enough for today', 'You've had enough', 'If you do that again …', 'It's time to leave' and, unfortunately, 'You can't go to the toilet there.' And, as with most drunks, it takes a toddler to fall asleep for the madness to end.

However, unlike drunks, a toddler has never in the history of parenting said, 'I'm so sorry for the hell I put you through today in the shop. I can't believe I acted like that. I was just very tired. I think I'll go to bed early tonight.' But, like drunk people, they also fall asleep in cars. Why do kids, especially babies, like cars? Some theories suggest that the noises and movement remind them of the womb; others say it relaxes the mind because nothing can be done until the destination is reached, so they allow themselves to fall asleep. Regardless, like thousands of other parents, we drive around aimlessly during the day, and sometimes at night, just to make babies and toddlers sleep.

In our case, on all our family holidays, we have to plan our journeys around 'nap time', which is mid-afternoon. We had no internet, so we looked at the opening times and directions on the map in the brochure. I figured out it would take around thirty minutes to get to Lahinch, or three minutes if the wind was behind us. The only thing was, we had five and a half hours to kill before we took off.

7:05 a.m.: After breakfast Olivia asked me if the fish in the sea know the fish in the aquarium. I said yes. For the next ten minutes, I had to explain how the fish get to the aquarium. I struggled with it and wasn't exactly sure how they did. It resulted in my wife butting in and telling her, 'They take the bus.' Olivia was fine with that answer.

7:15 a.m.: Olivia asked me again how the fish get to the aquarium and could she take the same bus. This resulted in me having an argument with my wife. 'I was trying to tell her how, but you had to butt in,' was how I started this particular row.

Lorna's response was, 'Olivia, the bus can only take fish.' Again, Olivia was fine with the answer.

7:35 a.m.: I was reading the ingredients of corn flakes on the back of the packet. It reminded me of going to school. I didn't get a great Leaving Cert, but I know what riboflavin is. Lorna was reading her book. Olivia asked us at least twenty times, 'When are we going to the aquarium?'

8:00 a.m.: Lorna said that she was going to the shop to 'take a break'. I started row number two of the morning. 'It's not much of a holiday if you have to "take a break" from your holiday.' Olivia wanted to go with her. I made the statement of the holiday. 'If you go the shop now, we will have nothing left to do for the rest of the morning.'

8:08 a.m.: Lorna and Olivia went to the shop. I seriously thought about driving to Shannon Airport and going somewhere sunny. I mentally prepared a pitch for Lorna on her return.

8:35 a.m.: They returned from the shop. I started my pitch, entitled, 'It's pissing rain, let's go to Spain.'

8:36 a.m.: Row number three. Lorna said that I wasn't giving this holiday enough time. I retorted by telling her the truth: 'I hate this f##king caravan and there's nothing to do here.'

8:48 a.m.: Olivia asked me why I was looking at the corn flakes box again. Instead of telling her that I'd nothing else to do because there was no signal, TV or even newspapers and that I was fighting with her mother, I told her I was going to make a magic robot out of it.

9:00 a.m.: Without Sellotape or scissors, the magic robot was terrible. In fairness to Olivia, she said it looked like a puppy, so she played with it. Lorna and I looked at a two-year-old playing with a mangled lump of cardboard, pretending it was a puppy. We had to do something.

9:06 a.m.: We all went to the shop.

9:15 a.m.: The rain was so heavy we didn't make it to the shop and had to turn back half way. When we got back to the caravan, Olivia told us she didn't like walking in the rain.

9:16 a.m.: We got into the car. Lorna was warming to my Spain idea. We decided to go to the aquarium three hours ahead of schedule.

9:45 a.m.: After taking the scenic route, we arrived in Lahinch. The wind was so high (it's right on the coast) that an outdoor sign for a café flew past the car as we parked. We literally ran for it towards the beachfront aquarium. We made it to the door and looked at each other in a 'we made it' kind of way. Drenched, we walked brazenly up to the reception desk and asked for three tickets for the aquarium. Only in Ireland would the response be 'There's no aquarium any more, only the pool, the aquarium's been closed for a few years.'

My initial response was 'A few years? But we just got this brochure yesterday.' She looked away, while grabbing a swim hat. 'Yeah, we need to get new brochures.'

I wanted to tell her that our entire holiday rested on this, I wanted to tell her that her flippant response was going to make my two-year-old ask a million questions about where the fish had gone if they aren't in the aquarium. I wanted to tell her that I didn't sleep the previous night because I was in a metal coffin on wheels. But all I told her was that we'd seen actual road signs for the aquarium on the way.

'Yeah, they should take them down.'

I was losing my mind. I wanted to scream. Why is Ireland so obtuse when it comes to rain? It rains every day on this poxy island and anything that can relieve our boredom has 'closed down years ago'. The irony of it all was that the swimming pool was packed with toddlers and parents trying to avoid the rain, just like us. Then I heard Olivia say, 'Daddy, we're in the aquarium.' I looked across to the little shop. It was full of swimming hats, fridge magnets, Peppa Pig armbands, Peppa Pig flip-flops, Peppa Pig flippers, even Peppa Pig insurance policies (not really) and in the middle, a tiny little rack of teddy bear fish hanging from a mobile. 'Look, Daddy, the aquarium.' You don't get a handbook on parenting, and that's a good thing, because if you did, I'm sure it would say, 'If your child thinks that five badly made fish toys is an aquarium, you should tell her that it isn't. Instead, drive her to the nearest one so she is not confused in later life.' But there I was, bitching about my shitty holiday and a two-year-old was just delighted, out of her mind excited, to see a few fish toys.

Lorna looked at me. 'You see, that's what I'm talking about. She's loving this, Bernard, and you're ruining it for her.' Oh, the guilt. The poor little thing. I decided there and then to cop on. This was going to be a brilliant family holiday. I was going to be New Bernard. New Bernard saw the positive in everything. New Bernard could make every situation a fantastic opportunity for fun. So New Bernard drove his soaked family to the local town of Ennistymon. The whole town was shut and it was only 12 p.m. We went into a little café, where we were told, 'We don't do the proper coffee after twelve, because Maureen, who does it, picks up her kids. We have Nescafé or we can sell you Kit-Kats or paninis.'

The old Bernard wanted to burst out screaming, 'No wonder there are no tourists here. Coffee isn't a luxury. I grew up in the eighties. I worked on farms. I cycled everywhere. We had two TV channels. I saw mass emigration from our village, too. We had no money. I wore hand-me-downs – and I only had older sisters. *Learn how to use the f##king machine.*' But New Bernard, with his amazing wife and daughter, laughed it off and sat in the car in the pissing rain eating ice creams. We then headed on to the Burren, a vast, empty limestone landscape with nothing to see only grey, wind-worn stone for miles upon miles. What better way could you spend a pissing wet day on your holidays? Olivia piped up with possibly the best description of the Burren: 'Why is the outside so sad?' The old Bernard would have laughed uncontrollably and rubbed it in his wife's face. But the new, positive, holiday Bernard told her that the outside wasn't sad – the outside just missed its friend, Mr Sunshine.

Then came the pièce de résistance of our County Clare holiday. We decided to go to Ennis, the biggest town in Clare, to buy … yes, you've guessed it … warm clothes. You know you're on to a winner when you're in a sports shop in August buying a hoodie and a windcheater in order to make sure you don't die from hypothermia getting from the shop to the caravan with milk.

On our way back to the caravan, Lorna started to feel sick. By the time we reached the caravan park, she knew she had a stomach virus. That night was to become what I called our 'helladays'. For the next twelve hours, she went from the bed to the tiny caravan toilet every ten minutes. It was awful. Olivia was crying. I was tired of being 'positive' and the sea was trying to kill us.

It got worse that night. At two o'clock in the morning Lorna woke me. 'The toilet is broken'. I love the fact that my wife thinks I can actually fix anything.

'Well, I don't know how to fix it.'

She looked at me with her bloodshot eyes. 'I need the toilet, but the tank is full - you'll have to empty it.'

'It's the middle of the night, Lorna, I don't even know where the tank is.'

She looked at me, grabbed a plastic bag with a Peppa Pig magazine in it and puked. Twenty minutes later I'd Sellotaped my iPhone, with its light on, around my head, like a coal miner, and put on all the clothes I owned. I'm a big fan of

Deadliest Catch. It's a programme about fishermen in the North Atlantic who brave furious storms in order to bring home the catch. When I stepped out of the caravan at 2 a.m. in the middle of that storm, knowing there was a possibility I was going to get covered in shite, I made those guys look like newborn puppies.

First, I had to find out where the tank was. I went around to the side of the van and I could smell it. I saw the little handle with a caution sign above it – DON'T LET TANK OVERFLOW. The only time you will ever see this sign is, of course, when the tank overflows. I grabbed the handle and twisted it. It released easily enough. I thought to myself that this would be a cinch. I'd be back banging my head off some secret drawer while trying to sleep in no time. I was pulling the tank towards me when it burst out from the bowels of the caravan. I got splattered from head to toe in shite. Now I don't know if you know this, but a large plastic tank of shite weighs a lot. The park's safe-removal area was about a quarter of a mile uphill, where the communal shower and wash area was. I contemplated just emptying it there and then and letting the Atlantic do its business, but I didn't. I dragged that tank of shite uphill for a good half an hour. In my mind, it was reminiscent of Tom Crean's Antarctic expedition when he walked through the freezing cold for thirty-six miles, sustained only by two squares of chocolate and a couple of biscuits. If he could do it, I could do it.

I reached the communal area around 3 a.m. I emptied our tank, stripped off my clothes and got into the showers, which were freezing. Washing yourself in a cold shower at 3 a.m. during a storm is bad, and it was, but when you're washing your family's shite off you, it's a glass-half-empty/glass-half-full situation. I walked back to the caravan clean, cold, but naked. Carrying the now-spotless tank, I reinserted it, left my clothes outside in a black bin-liner and jumped into the caravan. I had visions of my wife and child embracing me, making me hot soup and asking me about my shitty frozen adventures. Instead my wife said, 'What took you so long?'

The next morning, straight after checking to see if I still had all my fingers, I told my wife that I was leaving and that she could come with me to a hotel if she wanted. She agreed. My father-in-law came down that evening to collect his caravan. I told him about my heroic adventure and he asked me, 'Why didn't you just use the wheels?'

'What wheels?' I said. He brought me around to the side of the van, pulled out the tank and showed me the two little wheels attached to its base. It was so dark, I hadn't been able to see them, so I'd just dragged it uphill.

'Jaysus, how long did it take you to drag a full tank up there?' he asked.

'Oh, not long.'

'You must have been covered in shite.'

'Oh, no, not really,' I lied. As we drove off to a hotel, I could see the disappointment in my wife's eyes. She was upset with me, but more with her childhood memories. I wanted to say, 'I told you so,' but I let some of my own family tradition go instead and said, 'Let's stop at a shop.'

22. He dyed all my clothes and said it was an accident.

I hate housework, so it's a nice gift that I'm not allowed to help with the washing of any clothes, except my own. This is partly because we have a massive difference of opinion as to what should go into the washing machine and for how long. My wife is adamant that all whites should be separated and that colours get their own wash. Also, tea towels and bath towels get a separate wash as they are 'dirty'. I don't have time for this clothing apartheid and my main reason is that washing machines, and especially washing detergent commercials, scream at us that you can wash anything at any temperature. Every washing machine now boasts that you can wash everything, including the house cat, in it at thirty degrees and everything will come out sparkling. So why does my wife persist in maliciously separating everything? As far as I'm concerned, once it's in the wash basket, it's dirty. I just throw it all into the machine, press the one button I know and away you go.

As for the dryer, same thing. Again, my wife is persistent in her segregation policy. 'I'm not drying your big, hairy-arse beach towel with the kids' clothes, it's disgusting.'

I constantly retort, 'IT'S CLEAN. IT'S JUST BEEN THROUGH A WASH.'

We had a trusty dryer for years that eventually packed it in. We recently bought a brand-new German dryer that thinks it's a better human than us. We started to notice that the clothes were a bit damp after they went through a full cycle. On examining the handbook, it told us, 'The dryer senses that the clothes are dry enough for you to place them in an airing cupboard.' So now the dryer 'senses' things? When you try to put the clothes in for a longer time, it just beeps and says, 'Put them in the hot press, you lazy Paddy.' Also, if any piece of clothing has been outside for the night, my wife wants to put in the bin because 'rats will have been all over it'.

After a few close shaves, we eventually agreed that I wouldn't wash any of her or the kids' clothes. Yes, her clothes. You see, I didn't mind grabbing her few bits and pieces and throwing them into the machine – sure, I was going that way anyway – but there were a few incidents that went horribly wrong. Kids' socks are the Antichrist to white clothes. You think you've separated all the colours, but on one memorable weekend, my five white shirts came out pink all because of a single Paw Patrol sock.

* * *

If you have small kids, you'll know that, to them, all ordinary household appliances become the most amazing toy ever. Tadhg was so obsessed with turning the knobs and buttons on the washing machine, we had to get a bespoke anti-toddler guard made for the front of it. He once played so much with my mother's dishwasher that she told me that whatever he had done to it, it was still on two days later. After the fourth day, she had to call a plumber, who told her that whatever sequence of buttons he'd pressed, he'd put it into factory mode and it had checked every single washing cycle.

Olivia goes more for the imaginative everyday experience of turning Daddy's trips to the toilet into a Disneyland experience. 'What are you doing in there, Daddy? I want to come in.' Eventually, after tears and screams (hers, not mine) I have to let her in, followed instantly by Tadhg. They are obsessed with it. It's as if they are queuing up to go to Space Mountain. It's no wonder that Lorna washes them and their clothes while I do the food. It works, because we both know where we stand – and because I did destroy all their clothes one bank holiday weekend.

Lorna went through a blitz of dyeing her clothes. Because she's very petite, she finds it hard to get clothes that fit her, especially for work, so she started to re-dye some of her clothes to get more wear out of them before she threw them out. I'm pretty sure she got the idea from dyeing her wedding dress to use it as a regular going-out dress. She is also handy with a sewing machine and her hobby is making dresses and stuff for around the house. She also does all the DIY, but that's an entirely different, emasculating story. The weekend of the washing disaster, Lorna had brought the kids down to her home place for a long weekend. I was working, so I stayed at home. It was a perfect opportunity to throw out loads of stuff without her noticing. While going through the press in the washroom, I found purple clothes dye. I got a brainwave. I could dye all the white shirts that had gone pink because of the rogue Paw Patrol sock a nice shade of purple.

I got my shirts and put them into the washing machine. I didn't read the instructions on the dye pack, because as we all know, it's just powder, so I chucked it all in. I washed them and waited. Hey presto, they came out purple. Even though I was going to be the brunt of Barney the Dinosaur jokes, I now had five wearable shirts. Straightaway, I was hit with dyeing fever. 'What else can I dye?' I wondered. I searched the attic and found loads of stuff that could do with a dye. I decided on yellow this time, found some yellow dye in the press, threw it in and voilà, I had loads of new yellow clothes. This went on for a while, experimenting with various colours in an overwhelming cascade of joy. Then it dawned on me that I should dye all my Ireland away jerseys green. I threw them in and … as if by magic, green. I was delighted with myself. I spent at least half the day dyeing different clothes various colours. I had a new wardrobe and without having to try anything on.

While I was coming down the stairs with another load for the machine, I decided that I'd help out my long-suffering wife by washing some of her clothes. I had finished my multi-coloured adventures, so I just threw her shirts and blouses in a wash at 40 degrees and went to bed. The next morning, I decided to give her another surprise and wash the kids' clothes, so I dragged them downstairs to the utility room with me. I took out my wife's clothes, thinking that they looked a bit dark, but reasoning that it must be the wash, put them in the dryer, lumped all the kids' clothes into the drum, and, bing-bong bash, set the machine to forty and off it went.

Later in the day, I went to take my wife's clothes out of the dryer. They were all green. Everything. Her blouses, trousers, even her socks – all green. I'd never experienced panic like it before in my life. I didn't know what to do. Could I individually dye them all back to their original colour? Or did I have to go into town and buy a whole new wardrobe, implying that I like wearing petite women's clothes that look exactly like the ones I'd just COMPLETELY COLOURED GREEN?

I actually started to pray. I closed my eyes and for the first time in decades said, 'Dear Lord. I'm after dyeing my wife's clothes green. Please, when I open my eyes, put them back to their original colour.' I opened my eyes and they had turned back to their original colour. Oh, wait, no, they were still green, because God was punishing me for not praying, ever. I grabbed the box of dye. In bold lettering it was clearly stated: MAKE SURE TO WASH THE MACHINE SEVERAL TIMES WITH NOTHING IN IT BEFORE STARTING ANOTHER WASH. Instantly, I started thinking. I'd put on four washes: purple, black, red and green. Oh, no, the kids' clothes. They were a deep, disgusting black colour, all of them. Not alone had I destroyed Lorna's clothes, but also the kids': Olivia's favourite My Little Pony PJs now looked as if Twilight Sparkle had entered a cult of satanic donkey slashers.

I put the washing machine on with nothing in it to rinse it, then did what I normally do when I've completely messed up. I rang my mother. Google is fine, but I was working under extreme pressure here. I had roughly five to six hours before Lorna and the kids got back.

'Mammy, I'm after dyeing all of Lorna's and the kids' clothes different colours.'

She didn't judge, she just answered, 'You can buy a dye-remover that gets it all out, from the same place where she bought the original stuff.'

YES! 'Thanks, Mammy, bye.' Keys, car into town ... problem. I had absolutely no idea where she'd bought the dye. I was googling frantically, but it was telling me there were a myriad of different shops where dye could be bought. I had only one option. I had to call her.

My wife gets annoyed when I call her for no reason. In the past, she would regularly say things like 'Bernard, are you bored again, because I'm at work. I have a real job.' I used to get really annoyed because, yes, I was bored and most of my friends didn't get up until midday, so I'd want someone to talk to, but these days, I have an in. I can just say, 'How are the kids?'

I knew my first line couldn't sound panicky. 'Hey, how are you? Nothing strange up here at all. How are the kids?'

'Yeah, they're fine,' Lorna replied. 'What did you get up to for your free weekend?'

'Oh, just work, really.'

'Okay, I'll be up around three.'

'Lovely … eh, listen, before I let you go …'

I could simply have said something like, 'I'm thinking of dyeing some clothes – where did you buy the dye?' But I had to go for the most convoluted lie possible: 'Some of the lads were thinking about dyeing their football jerseys a different colour and were wondering where you could get dye to do that?'

There was a pause. 'Did you use my f##king dye, Bernard? You'd better have washed the machine out before you put on another wash.'

'No, I *didn't* use your dye, the lads were just wondering.' I have no idea why I used the phrase 'the lads'. I have a few small groupings of friends; I'm not a 'lad' and as far as I know, I've never been officially aligned with any group that even remotely call themselves 'the lads'. I would like to be one of 'the lads', but that opportunity for indoctrination has never happened.

Lorna smelled a rat. 'What are you talking about? Who are "the lads"?'

'You know, "the lads".'

'What lads?'

'The lads.'

'What are their names?'

'Lorna, it doesn't matter. I'll find it myself.'

'I'll be back around three. We don't want to come back into a mess.' I had been warned.

In town, I parked and googled, 'Where can I find a dye that gets rid of dye?' It just returned mostly American websites – no shop in Dublin. Then I remembered the ancient activity that has faded away and is only practised by strangers with no 4G connection. I decided to ask somebody. Yes, that's right. I forgot that we humans are still able to ask complete strangers a question. I took a deep breath and walked into Penneys. Not to be confused with JC Penney in the USA, Penneys is uniquely Irish. Think of a large clothing store. Now think of clothes that you would like to wear. Say you only have a small amount of money, €30 for example. Now, what if you could buy a complete wardrobe of clothes with €30 and still have change at the counter for a bag of Maltesers? Welcome to Penneys. Irish people take so much pride in it. It is almost a national rite of passage to be able to tell somebody that the coat they are admiring on you was from Penneys and cost fifteen quid.

You have to be careful asking for an Irish person's help. I always tell tourists that Ireland is like being in a big play. Most people know their lines and what character they are supposed to play. A tourist could ask a simple question of a local: 'Excuse me, where can I find an ATM, please?' Four hours later, they are in that person's house drinking tea and going partners on a horse. So when I asked a lovely woman called Marie where I could get dye that gets rid of dye, it turned into a play called

The Red-Haired Fella's Question.

The Red-Haired Fella's Question

A red-haired man in his thirties enters a well-known Dublin shop called Penneys. There is a woman called Marie behind the counter. She is kind.

Red-haired Man: Excuse me. I'm sorry. I know you don't sell it here, but do you know where I could find a dye that gets rid of dye in clothes?

Marie: A dye-stripper, you mean?

Red-haired Man: Yes, exactly. Thank God. I thought nobody would know what I was talking about.

Marie: I couldn't tell you, son, where you'd get anything like that. But hold on, I'll ask some of the girls. Angela, do you know where this fella could get some dye-stripper?

Angela approaches the counter, holding a stack of black polo necks.

Angela: Jesus Christ, it's like people just come in here to throw clothes around, Marie. I've a pain in me hole putting clothes back on the rails. Someone left an open packet of ham underneath a stack of maxi dresses, what are we dealing with, at all, at all? So what were you saying, this fella's looking for a stripper? Play your cards right – me break's in three minutes.

Angela and Marie start laughing. The red-haired man is uncomfortable.

Angela: You know, I'm not sure, hold on, I'll ask Tony. (*she shouts*) Tony?

The red-haired man mutters under his breath.

Red-haired Man: For fuuu sake.

Tony arrives at the counter holding a half-eaten packet of ham in his hand.

Tony: Look what I found under a load of dresses. Animals, I'm telling ya. Animals.

Marie: Angela was just saying. Here, Tony, where would this fella find some dye-stripper?

Tony: Well, if he plays his cards right, I'm doing nothing tonight.

Tony, Marie and Angela are all now in hysterics.

Tony: Hickey's across the road, son, they sell it.

Marie: Oh, yeah, of course.

Red-haired Man: Thanks very much.

THE END

This is what I love and hate about Ireland and being Irish in equal measures. We will never give a straight answer, only entertaining ones. I walked into Hickey's and bought six boxes of dye-stripper. I thought I'd get a strange look at the till, but nothing. I suppose if you're one of the few shops in Dublin that sells dye-stripper, you've seen it all before.

When I got home, I opened the washing machine. This time I didn't pray, but I hoped that maybe the last wash had washed out the green. It had not. I read the instructions on the dye-stripper box and threw Lorna's clothes in. I waited the fifty-five minutes and when the machine beeped I pulled open the door and I couldn't believe it. The clothes were back to normal. In fact, all the clothes looked the same. Of course they did. At what point did I not compute that the stripper would strip all the dye out of the clothes? This was worse than dyeing them all green. They were now completely colourless.

* * *

I waited until 3 p.m. and, sure enough, the family bounded in. The kids were excited to tell me their adventures, but Lorna just turned to me and said, 'Show me.' I showed her the clothes. She picked up a grey, washed-out blouse and said, 'I'm pregnant. We're going to have four children.'

I was a bit shocked and replied, 'Are you having twins?'

'No, Bernard … Olivia, Tadhg, the new baby and you.'

23. He hasn't an idea how to dress the kids. Pyjamas to crèche, Bernard?

When my wife goes away, the kids and I miss her a lot. The kids don't think I'm able to really look after them like Lorna does. The last time she went away for a night Olivia said, 'But Daddy, what if anything happens?'

'But I'm here,' I told her.

She thought for a little bit and said, 'But who's going to look after you?'

Lorna is convinced the kids think I'm the same as them. She's right.

I have tried disciplining them. I'm not a hippy-dippy dad at all, but for some reason they just don't take me seriously. One afternoon, they wrecked the couch with crayons, yoghurt and blueberries. I was so incensed by the mess, I shouted, 'GET OUT INTO THE HALL.' They tore out into the hall and within seconds, they had run back in. 'AGAIN, DADDY, AGAIN.' They thought it was a game. It is now an actual game we play called 'The Hall Game'. It's actually brilliant if you need to get stuff done. Even when I thought I was at the zenith of my parenting prowess they were impervious to it.

People have never been able to take me seriously, yet I think I'm quite a serious person. Some people just have an automatic air of authority; I have an automatic air of uncertainty. This is exceptionally useful if you are a stand-up comedian, but a massive minus if you're trying to have control over your children. Lorna's mantra is 'You don't wash them, dress them, or do bedtimes.' This is 87 per cent true, but I cook all their meals and I do 'No-Nappy Saturday' with them, so that counts. No-Nappy Saturday happened when the two of them refused to wear their nappies or underwear if I didn't give them Nutella on toast for their breakfast. I wouldn't give in, thus 'No-Nappy Saturday'. Lorna stopped this immediately, also 'No-Clothes Sunday' and 'No-Learning Monday'.

However, a source of open-ended joy that I constantly remind her about was the time I was right about letting the kids be bored. If you let a toddler be bored, they will eventually turn themselves into a princess, or ghost, or some sort of imaginary hybrid goat-fairy thing. It's what kids do. They have an inbuilt capacity to never let themselves get bored. When I asked Olivia one day what 'bored' meant, she told me, 'I dunno, is it something to do with not going anywhere?' Bingo. Kids don't need to go places all the time, because everything they love is in their home.

It's not like when I was growing up. Two TV stations, a record player – yes, a record player, not even a tape deck – and three sisters who didn't want to play with me, except if they got 'bored', when they would dress me up as a human doll and call me Betty. I used to get so bored sometimes that I would read the Yellow Pages, the directory that listed business names. By the time I was in primary school, I knew every single plumbing contractor in the Republic of Ireland.

To this day, I remember the ads for Irish Sugar, Maxol and United Distillers on page 167. The irony of the Yellow Pages in Ireland in the eighties was that nobody had any money to use its services. As for the phone book! I would be waiting for the day the new phone book would come into the house. I knew every country's flag, time zone and international dialling code, along with how many 'Jas Murphys' were in our area. There were a lot. My father used to get so annoyed if he caught me reading the phone books. I wish I'd asked him why, but I think it was because they were still a bit official and precious to a certain generation. If I drew in one or ripped a page, I might as well move out. Most young boys got caught with a copy of *Playboy* under the covers. I got caught reading the international dialing code for Yemen.

Looking back, most of my friends had computer games. I'm only slowly realising that maybe I was a bit odd. It's that oddness that I know my wife is wary of passing on to our children, but therein lies the cruelty and craic of having kids. For example, the two older kids just can't stand getting dressed and I know that's a trait genetically handed down to them from me. I hate getting dressed. It's up there with having to put a duvet cover on, or an ironing-board cover. I looked it up. It's called vestiphobia. According to Wikipedia it's 'The fear of clothing. The origin of the word vest is Latin (meaning covering the body or clothes) and phobia is Greek (meaning fear).'

I probably have 'kidavestiphobia', which is the fear of dressing kids. Why is it so difficult getting them dressed? Why have their clothes got those little silver snap fasteners that never press together properly? And why, when you do eventually get them dressed, do they manage to get some form of milk product all over them instantly? I've never needed to buy so much yoghurt in my life since my children arrived.

My biggest problem is that I cannot distinguish one item of clothing from another. The front of their tops look like the back and as for the difference between PJs and day clothes, I don't have a clue. One thing is for certain – all clothes look good on kids. I tried buying the same clothes as Tadhg for a while. Instead of them looking good on me, I looked like I was retiring into a haze of beige.

When you see kids in the supermarket in a princess dress or with one shoe on in a dinosaur onesie with a Bob the Builder hat on, that's my kids. I just cannot argue with them any more about their clothes. If they want to wear a Rice Krispie box to their cousin's christening, so be it. The stress of trying to dress them has taken years off my life.

On one wet miserable morning, however, my wife didn't see the funny side to my lazy couture ways.

My wife drops the kids to crèche. I generally pick them up. By 'generally', I mean I don't forget. Thank God, I've never yet been in a situation where I'm idly wondering if there's something I have to do ... then remembering, oh yes! My offspring. I've abandoned them. On this particular morning, my wife had a course in Belfast. She left early in the morning, so the task of getting the kids up and bringing them to crèche fell on my shoulders. And on my shoulders is where my kids were that morning, as that's where they wanted me to dress them – the logic being that Olivia wanted to get dressed like an adult, so she had to be the same height as one. I allowed her to pick out her own clothes. She came down the stairs in a pink My Little Pony suit. I looked at it and thought, 'Well, she's not going for a job interview, so why not?' An argument brewed, however. I thought that the pony was back to front, but she disagreed. We settled on a compromise and did it her way. I wouldn't let her wear her mother's high heels, though. Instead she got to wear her pink wellies that light up. I thought it was a sensible choice of footwear, as it was raining. She picked out a yellow rain jacket and over that she wore a bright pink gilet. She looked like a tiny bag lady, but we were on time, so I didn't care. I dressed Tadhg as per usual and we took off.

When we arrived at the crèche, we were greeted with 'Oh wow, Olivia's very stylish today.' She was overjoyed with her ensemble. I told the crèche that Lorna would be picking them up today, not me. When I got into the car I thought, what's all this fuss about dropping kids off? I completely aced it today.

At 5:15 p.m., my wife called me. Here is the FBI transcript of that call.

Lorna: Bernard...

Bernard: Yeah?

Lorna: Have you any idea how irresponsible that was?

Bernard: What?

Lorna: You know what.

Bernard: No, I don't.

Lorna: Olivia's clothes – how could you? She had to go outside in them and stay in them all day.

Bernard: What are you talking about? I put her in clothes.

Lorna: She was in f##king pyjamas, Bernard.

Bernard: No, she wasn't. She was in her My Little Pony suit.

Lorna: There is no such thing as a My Little Pony suit. They are her PYJAMAS.

Bernard: Well, I've never seen them before. She picked them out.

Lorna: She took them from the wardrobe. They don't even fit her – the tags were still on them. And worse, she had them on back to front.

Bernard: I told her the horse should face forward, that's not my fault.

Lorna: You sent her to crèche in PYJAMAS.

Bernard: It looked like clothes.

Lorna: And she had wellies. Where were her shoes? She had to wear wellies all day.

Bernard: She wanted to wear her wellies. It was raining.

Lorna: They are heavy on her feet. Bernard, you are irresponsible.

Bernard: No, I am not. She wanted to wear them, it was raining, she likes them. As for the pyjamas, they looked like clothes.

Lorna: Why was Tadhg wearing normal clothes then?

Bernard: Because I picked them out for him.

Lorna: We'll talk about this when we get home.

Bernard: There's nothing to talk about. Is she okay?

Lorna: Yeah, she's grand. She just had to stay the whole day in her PJs and wellies.

Bernard: Did she mind?

Lorna: No, why would she? She's four.

Bernard: Exactly – there's nothing to talk about.

Call ends.

I am not an irresponsible parent. I pay attention to what they wear. The problem here isn't me. The problem here is that children's pyjamas look like day clothes. It used to be very simple. The only time you saw a cartoon character on clothing was on nightwear. Now, they're on everything: lunchboxes, coats, wellies, shoes, duvet covers; whatever character your child likes, they can have it on whatever they like. Clothes are clothes, anyway. Her PJs probably kept her as warm as any other top she owns. This was going to be my defence.

When I got home, Lorna said that fantastic line: 'I'm not angry, I'm just disappointed.' If ever a sentence was undebatable, it's this one. It's the nearest thing to killing a person with words. There is no way to stop someone from being disappointed, if they are already launched-themselves-into-deep-space disappointed.

But it was then, in a moment of pure genius, that I asked, 'Who are you disappointed in?'

The response came quickly. 'You.'

'Great,' I said. 'I don't mind if you're disappointed in me. Every day, loads of people are disappointed with me. I'm used to it.' You're probably thinking what a useless response, but it's true, and not just for me but for everybody. Nobody has the capacity to please everybody all the time. For God's sake, this is part of an actual saying, and by Abraham Lincoln, no less. There is no point in being disappointed in other people, especially toddlers and old people, even though these are the two most vulnerable age groups. Why? It's simple. Toddlers are coming into the world and older people are going out. One group has yet to see what the world is all about and the other has seen it all. That's why children love Granny and Granddad so much more than their parents. Why? Because grandparents don't impose rules like 'You can't wear your pyjamas to school.' They understand that toddlers don't give a s##t what anybody thinks of them. Think about it: toddlers will say anything, cry anywhere, speak their minds fluently, wear anything, because they haven't experienced life or let stupid idiotic things like shame, guilt or self-awareness ruin them. Meanwhile, on the bus out of town, Granny and Granddad realise that it's just not worth sweating the small stuff.

'We're going to be one of those odd families,' my wife said later, staring into the television. Herein lay the crux of the matter. Lorna didn't want us to be the kind of parents who say that anything goes, that there are no limits to our children's self-expression.

'So what?' I said. 'What does it matter if we're the odd family?'

'You can't let her go out with her PJs on, Bernard. That is odd, you're odd.' And there was the truth.

'Yes, I'm odd and I don't care. Half the time it's everybody else who is odd, not me. The fact is, there are no facts, stuff just happens.' Things quietened down and then my wife pointed at Olivia and said, 'Fine, *you* get it off her.' It is one of the downsides of letting your child express themselves. It took me two days to get the back-to-front pyjama top off her. The one she picked out herself and wore for 48 hours. When I eventually did get it off her she said, 'Okay … what am I going to put on next?'

24. He never, ever remembers to put the bins out.

Kids get sick a lot. Exactly when you don't need them to. It's the one thing they don't tell you in the hospital. There should be a big sign when you leave with your baby, saying, 'You'll be back.' And the single biggest parenting mistake is not selling medication as a treat. Our kids just constantly ask for treats. These can range from Kinder eggs, to comics, to broccoli. A long as it's called a 'treat', they want it. The psychology of it is simple. A treat will make you feel good. So why, then, when you are trying to convince a three-year-old to take the Calpol that will make them feel better, do they shut up shop, or mouth to be more precise? The lengths we have gone to to give our kids medicine is ridiculous. I've resorted to dressing up as a princess and putting the little plastic medication syringe on the end of a wand and playing a complicated game of 'princess hospital' just so Olivia will take 5ml of an antibiotic liquid. Now, we all have to sit in a circle. We all have to pretend to take the medication and when it comes to whoever really needs it, we just hope and pray it goes down their gullet. This proves difficult as your oldest child sees the scheme for what it is and then tells the other child that they're being scammed. Every parent will have their foolproof way of getting the stuff into their kids, but this is the bottom line. We are programmed deep within our psyche not to like medicine. We should have told them that medicine was a treat from day one. If they can learn Spanish from watching Dora, they can learn to like amoxicillin.

Two eye-openers happened for us that eased our situation. My wife told me that on entering the crèche early one day to surprise Olivia and Tadhg, she saw them standing in a queue, waiting for Calpol. Apparently, when a child has to take medicine in the crèche, they are instantly cool. Children, like us, always want what they can't have, hence a queue for Calpol. Lorna exclaimed to all, 'Great! Now you'll take it at home for us.' And did they? No. However, something magical did enter our lives – unwittingly, through the anal passage. Yes, you have figured it out ... suppositories.

In Ireland, suppositories have never been popular, for children or adults alike. Yet on the continent, they regularly prescribe them. You could walk into a café in Paris and there would be two or three people there, all talking about Baudrillard and sipping coffee, while elegantly inserting suppositories into their derrières.

I have a theory that suppositories never took off here because Ireland was so Catholic and sexually repressed. It was almost like saying, 'Oh, by the way, you can get that in filthy dirty up-the-bum form.' Everybody talks about great inventions like the internet or NutriBullets, yet no one stands up and roars 'SUPPOSITORIES ARE AMAZING', especially if you have kids.

Olivia was our first – she suffered from high temperatures. The ear thermometer was basically a part of her outfit. We carried one and packets of paracetamol suppositories with us everywhere. Only a few short years earlier, before I left the house, I'd make sure I had my wallet, keys and glasses; now it is a homemade febrile-convulsion kit. The difficulty with suppositories is that they are dreadful to give, but at least you know they're in. They were a godsend for us. No more cleaning up spit and hate off the couch, or begging them to take the littlest of tastes. They are generally only given with paracetamol or ibuprofen, not for antibiotics. When I ask why you can't get antibiotic suppositories nobody knows the answer, but whoever invents them will be a millionaire. I'm thinking of studying medicine just to see if I can do it.

Along with our new posterior pal, I insist on water being the cure for all ills. That's what I got growing up. Bed and water. Anytime we felt sick, my father would just say, 'Have a glass of water.' I'm really glad we didn't grow up as nomads in the Sahara. Or 'Run it off.' You could actually be holding your leg in your arms and he'd say, 'Run it off.' They were definitely made of sterner stuff. So now, when I say to my kids to get a glass of water when they don't feel well, I know I've come full circle.

We are, however, gifted with a child who never gets sick. Tadhg. He screams out various foods in his sleep. He draws all over the walls and wants his meals served to him every three hours or God help you, but he rarely gets sick. The one time he did get a temperature, we were ready and experienced. I just inserted the suppository as I changed his nappy. I thought, this will be fine. There was an explosion. He roared. No tears, just a primeval roar. When I eventually got his nappy back on, he walked around the kitchen, holding his bum, occasionally glaring over at me again as if to say, 'You put something up my arse … didn't you?'

When my wife came into the room, he beckoned her over and started roaring crying, blubbering, 'Daddy put a crayon in me.' No wonder he draws on the walls. He wouldn't let me change his nappy for about six months.

I was delighted that I'd finally found a quick way of administering essential medicines. Little did I know that I would literally receive a dose of my own medicine.

I was booked on *The Late Late Show*, a big deal, especially for a comedian. However, without fail, every time I get booked for the Friday night live show, I get sick. Hence, on this occasion, on the Thursday night, I got, not 'man flu', which my wife told me I had, but the bubonic plague. I was so sick that my snot was blue. I was shivering and sweating at the same time, and I had no appetite – I know I'm really sick when I've no appetite (I'm a big man with a big belly). But it's too much of an opportunity to say no to, so I drove out to RTÉ studios on the Friday evening, hoping that I would magically get better. I didn't.

The booker rang me while I was trying to get out of my car. 'Where are you now, Bernard?' I wanted to tell him that I was dying and that they should bring me on as an historical re-enactment of what it was like to be sick in the 1500s, but I did the usual 'On my way.'

I couldn't believe what was happening to me. I couldn't get out of the car. I couldn't move my legs. I felt pain in my hair. I thought I was going to have to ring for an ambulance. Then I remembered I had a thermometer in the glove box. I reached in and pulled it out and stuck it in my ear. It read 39.9°. My other ear read 40°. I knew this was very bad. I tried to drink water, but found my throat was so tight it was hard to swallow. I couldn't cancel now, I thought, or I'd never be asked back.

Then I had it. The suppositories! I pulled out the packet. I'd normally give Tadhg one and Olivia two, so I thought I'd perhaps insert four. I know now that self-medication should never be done, but I was sweating Ebola in a car park and couldn't walk … needs must. I thought I'd better get some advice on dosage, so I rang my wife.

She answered with 'I asked you to take out the bin, it's pissing rain and I don't want to leave the kids in here on their own.'

I told her my predicament and my temperature and that the bins were not important right now. She dropped one of her pearls of wisdom: 'Why don't you just have some water, Bernard? Take 500mg of paracetamol. That should bring your temperature down and when you get back, take out the f##king bins.'

I opened the packet and took out one suppository. When you're putting them up your own bum them little bullets look an awful lot bigger. I went for it. As soon as it went in, I caught my reflection in the rear-view mirror as I rose so high with the pinch. All I could see was Tadhg's face looking back at me. It was the same expression he'd had that day.

Number two went in and I was about to put in number three when there was a knock on my window. 'Howya, Bernard, could we get a selfie?' I realised that I'd parked in the public car park and that there were audience members looking into the car. I rolled down the window and one of them, a lady, put her arm around my neck. She told me she was from Longford and hoped that there would be a prize for everybody in the audience. I am truly sorry to that woman if I came across as rude, but I couldn't speak. I know people travel for miles to do dodgy things in car parks, but hopefully suppository insertion never takes off as a fetish.

I eventually got the four in and waited. Five minutes in and I could move my legs, ten minutes later I was walking towards reception. Once in the building, I just lay down in the dressing room. I tried to drink water, but still couldn't swallow. I could talk, though, and that's all that mattered. Once I heard my name and walked out on to the set, I wasn't sick at all, as the adrenaline kicked in, but Jesus Christ on a bike, when I got back into the car after, I paid heavily for shoving those waxy wonders where the sun don't shine.

* * *

The next day, Tadhg and Olivia came through the door into my bedroom, Tadhg with his beaker – 'Daddy, you can have my water' – and Olivia with the thermometer. They checked me out and told me I was going to be okay. It was such a lovely moment, until Tadhg came back in with a bar of soap from the bathroom and tried to stick it up my bum.

I called my wife to ask her to take them away so I could get some sleep. I could hear her shout from downstairs. 'Get up.'

I shouted back, 'I'm really sick', to which her reply came quick and fast: 'If you can go on a chat show with a forty-degree temperature, you can take out the bins.'

25. I caught him stark naked in the kitchen, shoving ice up his nose.

As a child I constantly had a snotty nose. I had several nicknames: 'Candles', because of the two snots always hanging out of my nose; 'Snotsers' – self-explanatory; and my favourite, 'Prince', because I was constantly blowing myself. Apparently, the artist, in one of the most brilliant urban myths (in my case, it would be a rural myth) could blow another part of his anatomy with his ribs removed.

I hated my mother or father wiping my nose and they did it a lot. A big chunk of my childhood memories are nail-bombed with 'Bernard, blow your nose' or 'Come here to me, there's a big snot.' I still wake up in a cold sweat after having nightmares about some overused hanky bearing down on my face. Yet I feel the insane urge to blow my children's noses, much to their disapproval, on humanitarian grounds. The last time I tried to blow Olivia's nose, she screamed, 'It's not your nose to blow.'

The cuffs of my school uniform were destroyed by snot when I was a child. Why it never dawned on me, as a young boy, to bring tissues in my pocket to school is still unfathomable. When you picture the snotty kid in all those children's films, that's me. My mother thinks it's because I was fed through the nose in an incubator when I was a baby. I was two months premature, born in March but should have been born in May. The fact that they fed me through the nose for two months should have made the snot go the other way, I always thought. Someday, I'll do a medical exposé into it and hopefully find out that I'm a miracle human. This is my constant daydream. That somehow science reveals me to be some alternative species. This might explain my recent onslaught of sinus infections, which eventually led to me getting pneumonia (or the quasi-self-diagnosed pneumonia I described earlier).

It all began with a failed swimming experiment on the radio breakfast show. As you know, I only learned to swim in my thirties, even though I first started swimming lessons in school when I was six or seven. I eventually swam the width of a swimming pool three decades later. Once I started swimming, I took to it like a duck to walking. I was slow, I had very bad technique and my main priority was not to drown. Over the years, however, I've grown to love it and at one point swam nearly every day.

Enter another project that I would start but never finish. I decided to try to beat the very first Olympic hundred metres time. It was set by a Hungarian, Alfréd Hajós, in the 1896 Olympic Games in Athens, at 1:22.2. Bearing in mind that he did it in the Mediterranean wearing a cotton swimsuit, which in water would weigh a tonne, it was a real feat.

Swim Ireland set me up with a young professional swimmer and coach called Brendan, who met me every week for a month to train me for my attempt at the record. He designed a plan for me and fixed my stroke. I had access to a 50-metre pool close to my home. Everything was in place for me to do it … until I started getting sinus infections when I got out of the pool. I switched pools – same thing, a sinus infection straight away. I then developed a cough that moved into my chest and stayed there for months. I couldn't breathe. I knew if I said I was sick my wife would berate me for starting another project I couldn't finish, so I persevered. Eventually, I was prescribed antibiotics and steroids and told to stay away from swimming pools. Someday I will break that record, along with finishing the following:

* Walking the length and breadth of Ireland
* Learning to type
* Entering the Eurovision
* Doing an Ironman
* Getting a six pack
* Learning the piano, harp and accordion
* Going three rounds of a boxing match, and finally,
* Becoming a stonemason

The doctor also said that, if I had to swim, I should nasal cleanse first. Being a man who just loves fads and self-experiments, I decided to google 'nasal cleansing'. Somehow what was once a regular activity practised by all humans has gradually morphed into the world of alternative medicine, in the guise of small, overpriced pottery teapots called 'neti-pots'. I began to see neti-pots everywhere and eventually bought one.

The lady in the shop told me how to use it. She had a mix of Polish and Irish accents and she warned me, 'Don't have the water too hot, okayay?'

'Yes,' I said.

'Booot don't 'ave it too cauld,' she went on, 'because the salt won't dissolve.'

'The salt?' She told me that I needed to mix a little bit of sea salt with the water. It helps with the cleaning. She also went into great detail as to how to get the water to go into one nostril and out the other, while bending over and turning your head to the side at an angle. Off I popped home with my massively overpriced tea pot – €25 – and a bag of Himalayan sea salt, which was also competitively priced at €15. I'm still at pains to find the Himalayan Sea.

I left them on the shelf in my shower and there they lay until months later.

My in-laws were staying with us one Friday night and on Saturday morning, they got up with our children. This was a godsend, as it meant I could take a shower alone. Small children seem obsessed with following adults into bathrooms. With them occupied, I could take a leisurely shower. I spied my neti-pot and decided that this morning was the morning for its trial. I boiled a kettle and put the salt into the neti-pot. I knew it would be too hot to use straight away, but my plan was to let it cool down while I finished my shower. I love the shower. If I could stay in the shower for the rest of my life, I would. It must be the nearest we get in adulthood to the experience of being in the womb. Instead of going through extensive psychoanalytical therapy, all you have to do is turn the immersion on for half an hour.

There I was, all alone, enjoying the simplest of pleasures. No one bursting the door down, asking what I was doing, or telling me that her brother looked at her in a bad way. It was my time to enter the hippy-dippy world of nasal cleansing. There I stood, as nature intended, naked, with a €25 mini-kettle in my hand. I shoved it up my nostril, bent over and HOLY CHRIST. Not alone was it scaldingly hot, but my eyes, what was happening to my eyes? It was like somebody had punched me in the face from the inside with the torch used to burn Joan of Arc at the stake. I roared and quickly tried to cool down the inside of my nose. You have no idea how difficult that is. If you've ever burnt the inside of your nose, you'll know there is no way of getting anything to stay up there. Eureka! Ice.

I ran out into the kitchen and got ice from the machine in our fridge. I know some people take great pleasure in shoving certain substances up their nose, but the relief I felt was instantaneous. Then I realised that my in-laws, wife and children were staring at a naked man shoving ice up his nose.

'Bernard, what are you doing?' My wife was screaming at me, the kids were laughing and my poor in-laws were pretending to look at anything bar me.

'I had the water too hot in my new nasal-cleansing device and the neti-pot burnt my nostril,' is what I thought I said, but apparently, because the inside of my face was being cremated, I said, 'hehin hide huff mo foce is nurning'.

She pushed me back into the bathroom. 'Hill hu ring me ring rice?' I said, thinking I was asking her to bring me in ice.

'Just dry yourself, you f##king eejit.'

I had burned the inside of my nose so badly I couldn't breathe out of my right nostril. Breathing is really important. It's up there with eating and sleeping, apparently. I had to bring a little bag of cotton wool and a bottle of water around with me for days. I would wet the cotton wool and shove it up my nose, accompanied by agony; however, it would only eliminate the pain for about five minutes, when I had to repeat the exercise again.

Here's one thing I found out. There are next to no products on the market for burnt nostrils. The shame of having to ask in several chemists and, of course, answering the constant question 'How did you …?' It was easier asking for condoms as a teenager.

Around this time, Lorna was pregnant with our second child and Olivia would sleep with me at night. Her go-to comfort zone is to hold my nose as she sleeps. I've found out that this is quite common. It's just incredibly painful when you've burned your nose. I had two options. Get no sleep with her squeezing it and me being in pain, or sleep with no pain. I chose sleep. But life seems to attack me in twos not threes. I got a sinus infection. Try blowing your nose when it's so burnt and raw. It looked like a scene from Omaha beach in 1945 in miniature. I couldn't blow my nose, so I had to let the snot build up and let gravity take its course. The mucus, however, helped the pain, as it worked like a quasi-protective layer. I started thinking about coming up with a new product that would mimic it for the unfortunate people who'd been mangled by neti-pots.

My wife asked me, 'So, you're going to try and invent snot?' It's another invention that might sit on the shelf for a while.

The following Saturday morning I awoke to pain again. Olivia had woken before me and now sat on my head with a tissue in her hand, trying to blow my nose. When I eventually got her off me, she looked at me, took a deep breath and shouted, 'You see, Daddy, nobody likes it when they aren't allowed to blow their own nose.'

26. He does absolutely nothing with the kids and he says that boredom is 'good' for them.

My earliest memories involve my sisters treating me like a human doll. They dressed me up in a yellow dress one Saturday. They did my hair and make-up and walked me into the village. They called me Aoife and said I was their daughter. I was only about four, but I remember meeting one shopkeeper who asked me what my name was. I told him, 'I'm Bernard, but if you see my sisters, tell them I told you I was Aoife.'

When my father found out, he thought it was the funniest thing in the world; however, my mother was furious. What really hits me about my day as a girl, or should I say, as Aoife, was that nobody in the town batted an eyelid. Pranks like these were common occurrences with my sisters. What's more, I didn't mind. The fact that they were playing with me was enough. It's lonely being the only boy.

Fast forward to my own son, who would do anything to join in with Olivia's games. The difference between Tadhg and Olivia was minimal at the start when it came to playing with each other. Olivia would dress as a princess and Tadhg would normally copy her by becoming a prince, but as he got older, he always became a dragon who would destroy everything and anything she had built. Tadhg, like most small boys, can be extremely affectionate. He loves his mammy and daddy, but there is only one true love in his life. Tadhg loves food, so much so that he wakes in the middle of the night shouting out random meals he would like. Even when he gets a banana he has to sit down at the table with a spoon and fork. It's quite frustrating as he doesn't do snacks – he will only eat formally. It's like he's a 1920s gentleman who wants his meals prepared and presented to him perfectly and consistently.

He also loves watching me cook. At first, it was nice, but then became a pain as he wanted to get into the oven, mix everything and basically make a mess. I know you're supposed to make 'a positive environment' for your children, but if you have to clean it up afterwards, that takes the positive out of it for me. Tadhg is particularly obsessed with flour. Every so often Olivia and Lorna bake and once they've weighed it out we have to hide it, as he keeps wanting to push his hand through it and basically spray it everywhere, like a bottle of champagne.

One Sunday afternoon, Lorna and Olivia went to a show together on a day they called 'mummy–daughter day', so myself and Tadhg decided to have a big daddy–little daddy day. Tadhg loves being left alone with me. Not because I'm great fun or adventurous, but because I do the one thing he loves … nothing. I don't wash him, I don't try to clean his nose or hands, I don't say no to anything, unless it's going to kill him, and I'll give him whatever food he wants, except chocolate. Basically, we enjoy the same thing: being left alone.

My mother told me that as a child she could leave me in a room for hours and I would entertain myself. On myself and Lorna's first ever transatlantic trip, she was genuinely shocked that I sat in a seat for seven hours with nothing. No TV, no iPod, books, films, nothing. I just sat doing nothing for seven hours. I love doing nothing and, by nothing, I mean nada, zilch. I'm not meditating, or being mindful, I'm just doing nothing. My mind is blank, taking a break. I just enjoy being lazy. You can do this on an aeroplane, as it's hard to do the shopping or empty the dishwasher. If you ever want to become less stressed out, just sit and do nothing. No breathing techniques or visualisation – just beautiful blank, bare, boring nothing. It works.

Me and Tadhg sat for hours doing very little, until he said, 'Daddy, I want to do something.' That generally means one thing – rooting through the kitchen presses. This does my head in. What do small children think is in there? I remember, growing up, that if anything was lost in our house, my mother would say, 'Did you check the press?' Every house in Ireland has a press with junk in it. Plastic bags, tea lights, used batteries and a broken light fitting that you can't throw out because you need it to show the sales assistant in B&Q, who will know exactly where the replacement is. Kids just love rooting. Even though they have ergonomically designed toys that have been crafted through years of childhood development studies, they still want to play with an old phone charger and a bag of cable ties.

Tadhg knows I hate it when he starts opening the presses, so he quickly shut one of them when he saw me looking at him. He caught his finger in it. He was screaming, 'MOY FONGER'. I couldn't console him. I was kissing it and saying, 'Now is it okay?' It's probably one of those bad family traits we're going to hand down to our kids. When they fall, we kiss the offending body part, whether it be the knee or an eye socket, and then say, 'Okay now?' I'd hate to think that if they ever have an accident when they're older they'll ask the paramedics to 'kiss it better and get me a Kinder Egg'. I offered Tadhg chocolate, broccoli, all the big hitters, but all he wanted was ... flour.

I gave in and got him a little bowl with some water in it and covered the floor with a newspaper. He stopped crying and his pain went away. He started to do his party piece, mixing water with flour and making a gunk that he squishes between his fingers. He gets so much joy and pleasure from it. There he sat, just squeezing his disgusting little dough on the floor like a little dirty Buddha.

I left him for less than sixty seconds to go to the toilet and when I got back the kitchen, living room and front room were destroyed.

I had left the bag of flour on the kitchen island. He had done a toddler bridge to get up and grab the entire bag. (A toddler bridge is when they grab their little chairs, potties, whatever they can get their hands on, and build death-defying Cirque du Soleil bridges to reach things.) He had quite literally flung it everywhere. He had previous with the flinging of things, generally food: plates of broccoli, cabbage, once an eight-ounce steak that I found weeks later, half-eaten, in a Paw Patrol backpack. This was his first foray into flour-flinging, however.

It was in every crease of the house. Skirting boards. Hinges. Inside drawers. It was even on the inside of open packets of crackers inside presses that were shut. It looked like he was working in a cocaine factory that had just been busted by an over-zealous squad on *Miami Vice*. It took me four hours to clean it up but, worst of all, I knew I had to bathe Tadhg. He hates baths. Did I tell you he hates baths? He hates baths. I didn't want our day ruined by doing the one thing he pleads with us not to do to him.

When I tried to bring him upstairs, he was like a man being dragged down to a dungeon for a crime he didn't commit. Begging me, 'No, Daddy, no, please.'

I had to do it. I washed him. It was not pleasant. It took a lot of persuading to let me wash the suds out of his hair. I swear, the neighbours must have thought there was a murder happening. Eventually, when we got back down stairs he wouldn't talk to me and just grunted 'Dora'. I put *Dora the Explorer* on and we sat in silence.

When Lorna and Olivia got home, Lorna asked Tadhg how his day had been with Daddy. In his first-ever full sentence he told her, 'I'm not staying with Daddy ever again.' Lorna started to hassle me as to why he was so upset. There was no way I was going to tell her that I let him play with flour and that he'd flung an entire bag all over the house. Instead I just said, 'I don't know, he was fine up until now.'

Then Lorna said, 'Okay, guys, time for your bath.' Tadhg screamed, 'No, I had my bath!'

'Don't be silly, Tadhg, Mammy will be really quick,' Lorna said. He started pointing at me: 'Tell Mammy, Daddy, tell Mammy.' Lorna quizzed me again. I couldn't give in. I told her I didn't know what he was talking about.

'I didn't bathe him,' I lied. 'I hate bathing him.' But, as he went up the stairs for a second time in one day, screaming and blubbing, I broke. 'Stop. That toddler is innocent … he's had his bath.' I explained what had happened and the flour fiasco.

Lorna looked around. 'I should leave you two together more often. He's clean and the house is spotless.'

Tadhg hasn't played with flour since.

27. He called me back from my first night out with the girls after Tadhg was born.

The first time I had to look after Olivia and Tadhg (who was only a small baby at the time) turned out to be one of the most stressful nights of my life. Lorna's mom group had planned a night out. She had told me, no, warned me, about it weeks in advance. 'Bernard, do you want my mum to come up and help you?'

'No,' I told her. I genuinely thought I had this whole parenting lark nailed.

Lorna got ready and Olivia started to ask questions. 'Who's going to mind us when Mammy goes?'

I looked at her quite sternly. 'I am.' I never thought in a thousand years I would get the reply I got. She instantly wrinkled her nose and tilted her head and snapped, 'But who's going to look after you?' There it was in a nutshell. A three-year-old asking me, 'Who's going to look after you?' Olivia might love me and come into my bed every night for cuddles and hugs, but when it came to the reality of 'no Mammy' around, she was worried.

I reassured her that we'd have a great time. She came back again: 'I know that, but what if anything happens?' Again, I told her I was an adult and was more than equipped to deal with any eventuality.

* * *

There is one thing that my wife does that does my head in, and that's goodbyes. She has to make the goodbye bit too long. I allocate at least half an hour for Lorna's goodbyes. Maybe it's an Irish thing, but this whole 'Let's start a new conversation at the door as you're leaving' or 'Waving at the window as the car drives by' drives me mental.

Now, it was time for her to leave for her night out. 'Do you want them to cry for you, Lorna?' I asked, 'because if you just slip out the door, they won't even notice you're gone.' She actually agreed with me and slipped out the front door. Within seconds of the thud of the front door closing and me entering the kitchen, Olivia and Tadhg were in hysterics. Operation Sweets and TV was not working on Olivia and she screamed the house down, demanding that she 'SAY GOODBYE TO MAMMY'. Tadhg was just wailing. I didn't know what to do. Even though myself and Lorna had negotiated a truce on watching *Peppa Pig* during recent peace talks with Olivia, I broke and quickly found the pink piggy mind-destroyer on Netflix. In fairness, the pig did its job and Olivia settled. However, Tadhg did not. A full hour into my first posting as sole protector of my kin, I was failing miserably. Olivia was sugared up on Kinder bars and juice, happily watching Peppa, but Tadhg was still crying. I had tried everything. I had changed him. Given him a bottle. Winded him. Walked him in my arms, in the buggy, everything. Olivia was telling me that Mammy had said he was 'continated' earlier that day. When I said, 'Do you mean constipated?' she said, 'Yeah, that.' When you're getting advice from a three-year-old, you know your human satnav is off-course.

Eventually, after a full two hours of inconsolable crying, he fell asleep. I was overjoyed. The thought of something being wrong with him or, worse, having to call Lorna back from her night out filled me with dread. Within ten minutes Olivia was asleep on the couch. I put a blanket over her and sat back with Tadhg asleep in my arms. The sudden realisation that I could watch anything I wanted filled me with excitement. I looked at the programmes stored on my set-top box. There were two episodes of *Game of Thrones* that I hadn't watched. I sat back, but as soon as the intro titles kicked in, Tadhg woke again, but this time it was different. He was screaming. Not crying, screaming. Unbelievably, Olivia slept soundly through the racket. Toddlers have that ability. They have no guilt or shame built up in their brains from years of embarrassment and disappointment, so when they sleep, they just go for it. Forty-five minutes into the screaming, I felt like waking her up and asking her for advice because Tadhg had turned red.

I had two options: call an ambulance, or, worse, call Lorna back from her first night out with the girls. I thought, what would be worse: if she came back and saw an ambulance in the front drive, or to momentarily bring her back from a nice glass of Prosecco? I rang her. 'I'm sorry, he won't stop crying and he's red.'

When she came back, Lorna was angry, very angry. 'I can't believe you called me back.' She took one look at Tadhg and said, 'He's constipated, Bernard.' She took him off me, did the legs thing and within a few seconds I could hear a grunt and then the show was over.

'Jesus Christ, Bernard, you called me back home from a night out because he needed a poo?' I tried to explain, but all she saw was *Game of Thrones* on the telly.

'Is that what you want? To watch your stupid dragon programme?'

Now wasn't the time to argue that the dragons weren't the essential element of the George R.R. Martin fantasy masterpiece. Instead, I told her, 'I was going to call an ambulance. I was freaked.'

Eventually she calmed down and I started into my Apology Quest. My Apology Quest goes like this: I start out at the Castle of Regret, then move through the scary Forest of Defensiveness, then into the tricky Lakelands of Denial and finally row my way carefully into the Land of Forgiveness. Eventually she realised that I hadn't called her back because I wanted to watch *Game of Thrones*.

'Go back to them, you'll only have been gone an hour,' I said.

'I can't go back, Bernard … I'm embarrassed.' Ouch. Now it was a two-fold issue. My wife thought I was a useless idiot and so did seven other women whom I'd never met. I needed to tell them about my predicament. I contemplated maybe going back to the restaurant and pretending I was a waiter and listening in to their conversations. Now, to several women, I was a f##king eejit. I was that guy that other women thank God they're not married to. Now, I'm that husband who is 'useless with the kids'.

But I'm not. I'm just not good with babies. I can entertain toddlers all day. I get toddlers. I get their rage and joy in equal measure. I get their single-mindedness in accomplishing tasks that have no use whatsoever. It's babies I can't handle. When they cry, I think, 'Oh no, there's something wrong.' They can't answer you back or tell you anything, but they seem to have a superpower, which is knowing where Mammy is every second. I feel for Lorna because she has cared so diligently for our kids, but once they started walking, they noticed me and I was like a big nightclub entrance to them. Club Daddy is where they can do nearly almost anything they want – within reason – while Lorna has to look on, thinking, 'Hello? I literally reared you.'

The next day I told Lorna I would babysit the kids for the whole day. Again, she pointed out, 'You don't babysit your own kids, Bernard.' However, that evening she went to the cinema without me. This was a blow. I love the cinema. She knows that. She then went on to tell me she goes to the cinema all the time without me. I was devastated. Everything I knew about her was destroyed. 'I'd prefer it if you had an affair,' I told her. 'How often do you go? Once, twice, how often?'

'Maybe three, four times a month.' I didn't feel quite so bad then.

Eventually Lorna went out with her mom group again. Luckily, Tadhg wasn't constipated or 'continated', as Olivia would say. But only half an hour into Lorna's absence, Olivia went missing. I knew where she was. When she's quiet, she's always in one place, her mother's wardrobe, trying on her heels. I ran up the stairs and right enough, she had raided her mother's shoe collection, like Imelda Marcos. She got a shock when she saw me and twisted her ankle on one of the heels. She started to bawl but it was one of those cries to get out of trouble as much as actual pain. Eventually, I asked her if she was in pain.

She said, 'Yes, a little.' Then she stopped, rubbed her nose with the butt of her hand and said, 'But not bad enough to call Mammy back from her night out.' Women understand pain.

28. He's hopeless at DIY, but he won't let me do it. He says it's emasculating. And he once used a condom to fix the pipe under the sink.

My problem with DIY is that my brain knows what to do, but my hands won't do it. This goes for dancing, sports and generally all physical activities. I once put up a shelf for my wife that was okay, as long as she didn't put anything on it. I tried to explain to her that where she wanted it (in the bathroom) was only plasterboard and if anything heavy went on it, it would break off. This shelf is still used as an example to berate me on my home-improvement skills to this day. The good things I achieved in the DIY department are never discussed. I fixed our fridge, for example. Yes, with a blow torch; but I had to. The freezer over-froze and pushed out a piece of plastic, which made the door not close properly. So I borrowed a blow torch and melted the bit back in. It worked – about 60 per cent. The door closed, except it had to be held in with three belts I'd tied together. Okay, every time you opened or closed it, you had to do or undo its belts, but it still worked and it felt like I had given the fridge human qualities. I called him Frederick. Frederick the Fridge. My system was working fine, until my wife saw that I had used two of her belts and that was the end of that.

Lorna never talks about the time I successfully rewired a hairdryer to support an Irish plug, not an American one. Instead of her having to use an adapter all the time, I fixed it. Yes, it exploded and somewhat went on fire, but I still fixed it.

She never talks of the time I fixed a hole in the wall with Polyfilla. She has to keep mentioning that I also used Sellotape and a staple gun, but that is beside the point. Where there once was a hole in the wall, there now isn't and I only have to replace the Sellotape twice to three times maximum a year.

Yes, I am lethal at any form of improvement, self or home.

There is a saying in the building trade: 'measure twice, cut once'. That should really apply to me and my drill: 'level twice, drill once'. But when it comes to buying drills, I'm like a six-year-old in a toy shop, except that I now have money and can get what I want. As for Aldi and Lidl selling them! Nothing gives a man more pleasure than being able to buy a head of cabbage and a power tool in the same shop. A drill in my hand is dangerous weapon. A dangerous, uneven weapon. Whatever I drill is never straight, but it's not my fault. Whose fault is it? I'll tell you: EVERY IRISH BUILDER.

During the building boom in Ireland prior to 2008, apartment blocks were built quicker than Lego sets. When the downturn happened, I thought, here's a great opportunity for all those builders to come back and finish what they started. Every person I know has a litany of problems that come with having to live in the worst accommodation with the pleasure of having had to pay the highest price. Here is my top ten list of dreadful building practices, partly from my own experience. Read this like you're counting down the top ten songs on *Top of the Pops*. If you were born after 1990, you will have to google *Top of the Pops*.

At number ten. Skirting boards. Forget about hammering them into place – just glue them onto the wall. This will give the buyer the added bonus of thinking they live in zero gravity, as nothing seems straight and the room appears to be floating.

At number nine. Heating pumps that double up as constant alarms because they are so loud. That's right, when anybody in your apartment block runs a shower, you'll know about it, as will anybody within a five-mile radius. Here in Ireland, we pride ourselves on installing the cheapest and loudest pumps in the world.

At number eight. Washer-dryers. Have you built an apartment block that's so small each unit barely meets the European requirement? Don't worry! Save on space by installing a washer-dryer. Give your tenant the pleasure of receiving a massive electricity bill and never having dry clothes – ever.

At number seven. Studio apartments. Want to give your bedsit a better name? Well, why not call it a 'studio apartment'? You'll also be able to charge twice the rent.

At number six. Listenable walls. Yes, why pay costly phone bills to call your neighbours when the walls are so thin you can hear everything that's happening around you, from boisterous love-making to the all-night-long arguments of the German couple living above you?

At number five. Magic toilet seats. Are you sick and tired of regular toilet seats, ones that you can just sit on? Well, why not come to Ireland, where every toilet, for some magical reason, swings to the left.

At number four. No storage. Do you own one of those big, awkward suitcases that you put your stuff in when you have to travel? Well, get rid of it because in an Irish apartment there is absolutely no stupid storage taking up space. The only thing you'll fit in your flat is your constant disappointment.

At number three. Like taking a hot shower? Like taking a cold shower? Good, because here in Ireland we've decided to make showers that either scald the skin off your bones or freeze you into hypothermic joy. If you want to have a mix of hot and cold, even, dare I say, a lukewarm shower, you're in the wrong country.

At number two. Want to raise a family? Well, have we got an awesome idea for you! We have designed every block of apartments in Ireland to be next to impossible to get a buggy, or a child, in or out of. As for packing your car, well, because we charge you twenty grand for a car-parking space nowhere near your front door, you're going to have to teach your child the urban art of parkour and watch them bounce off walls to get to crèche.

But at number one, and staying there for the next decade, is your address. That's right. Why be one of those boring people who have an address, like No. 22 Bowler Street, or Flat 6, Basin Street Upper? We've decided to give everything the same name as the more expensive area miles away from you. Just so that when you order a takeaway, you can have a friendly three-hour chat with the driver who's trying to find you. So, when your food arrives it's stone cold … yum.

Now that I've got that off my chest, the most disastrous experience anybody will have with DIY will be plumbing. Even handy people say, 'Stay away from water.' And as I'm distinctly un-handy, I didn't listen, which led to one of my more toe-curlingly embarrassing DIY episodes.

I had accidentally weakened a plastic pipe under the sink in our flat by pouring hot oil from the frying pan down the plug hole. I noticed it a few days later, as water was beginning to leak onto the floor through the press under the sink. On close inspection with the torch on my iPhone, I could see that it was a simple fix. All I needed was something that would seal the inner part of the pipe but also let it move. All I had to do was push the pipe up and seal it.

I put a biscuit tin under the U-bend and it worked brilliantly. It pushed the pipe up, but it didn't fix some of the water leaking out of the seal. If I'd known then that plumbers use a substance called sealant, I would have bought some, but I didn't. I stared at it for hours and eventually worked it out. A condom. I would take the pipe apart, roll a condom between the two pipes, then push the two pipes together with the aid of the biscuit tin. It worked. I ran the water for fifteen minutes and the press was bone dry. Not alone did I save us hundreds in plumbers' fees, we also had the first safe-sex U-bend in the world.

I knew Lorna would not be happy with my genius aqua-latex hybrid, so I told her the truth: 'I called a plumber and he fixed it.' It worked perfectly well for over a year, until we had to replace our washing machine. Now, I did break the washing machine by trying to wash an umbrella in it, but I did replace it. I wasn't there the day the shop came to install it. Unbeknownst to me, the installer pulled out the biscuit tin. Over the next few days, water built inside the condom and without any support underneath, it began to bulge out.

Then Lorna opened the press door. 'Bernard – what the f##k?' When I looked under the sink, the condom had grown to epic proportions. We were both looking at this water bomb under our sink. It was like a scene from a movie when they don't know what wire to cut to disengage the bomb and the countdown timer is at three ... two ... I went to turn off the water and it burst. Water went everywhere, along with bits of worn prophylactic.

That night, after Lorna had lectured me on how dangerous it was to use a condom to fix our plumbing, all I could think of was that everybody in the complex could hear her giving out to me. The next day I called a plumber. He came and looked at it and said that somebody had stuck a 'bleeding condom down your pipe'.

I did the right thing and told him the truth: 'I bet you it was some of the lads messing.' Lorna then did the unimaginable to a man's ego. She told the man what I had done. He thought it was the funniest thing in the world. I laughed along with them, but inside me, a pipe of internal tears had burst.

'Even if you're handy, you should never go near water, or plumbing,' he said, like a battle-hardened US marine standing at the door of the flat. He might as well have grabbed Lorna and kissed her in front me, so humbling was the experience. He had one last little dig, though: 'I'd hate to see what you'd fix the electrics with.'

Lorna replied. 'Well, at least I'd smell the rubber then.'

* * *

So I think we've established that I'm dreadful at DIY. My wife, on the other hand, isn't and recently did a DIY course. Did this threaten my masculinity? No. I do the cooking, so in my mind we're even. However, when it comes to buying furniture, we argue a lot. Lorna constantly watches mostly American TV programmes where families live mortgage-free in tiny houses with little to no overheads and very few possessions. So, when it comes to buying furniture, I'm always asking the question, 'Do we need it?'

The argument then goes: 'You're obsessed with de-cluttering, but won't stop buying things' (me).

She retaliates with 'You have more things than I do.' It goes on like this for quite a while, until one of the kids steps in, demanding a yoghurt, and we all sit down and watch our lives slowly slip away watching *Paw Patrol*. I get the tiny-house movement, but I do like things, unfortunately; expensive things. Even Lorna would admit that I stick to the old adage 'buy once and buy well'. I wear the same clothes until they wear out, simply because I'm comfortable in them or because they are of decent quality in the first place. However, I do constantly get slagged by friends over this. I once wore the same T-shirt, jeans and jacket combination for *seven years* on *Republic of Telly*. I never had to worry about continuity, but I was washing the same T-shirt four times a week. Now, I seem to unconsciously fill my life with tat. Amazon.com and sugar are my go-to dopamine playgrounds. This lethal combination has had a detrimental effect on my bank balance and my waistline.

But when my wife said that she needed a desk and that we should head to Ikea to get it, my *substantia nigra* went into overdrive: the thought of buying furniture and Swedish candy just made life seem so unbelievably exciting for a few hours.

Ikea is where all families eventually end up, looking for an answer to life's most important questions, slavishly dragging their young children behind them, while Dad generally either measures feverishly or looks at football results on his phone.

There are several types of 'Ikealanders', the name I give to people who end up in this screw-and-bolt landscape.

There are the Draggers. I'm a Dragger. A Dragger is someone who doesn't want to be there and is just dragged along. They will eventually start a fight with their spouse by reiterating how little they care about the functionality of a suction shower shelf and generally, they are the ones who end up sitting on one of the couches with a toddler, watching Netflix.

Then there are the Grand Designers. They have notebooks and pencils with them. They write down furniture codes on the little yellow note pads provided by Ikea and then take photos with their iPhones at strange angles. They also have measuring tapes – not the little ones Ikea leave out, but their own personal ones, which can measure a whole self-built Ikea flat. They mean business and generally end up buying a sock tidy.

Then there are the Nothingelsetodoers. The Nothingelsetodoers have nothing else to do. This group falls into several sub-categories. Some just aimlessly wander around, minding their own business, but others actually make the staff find things out, or take up the kitchen designers' time.

Finally, there are the 'Anti-Arrow-Walkers'. These are the renegades, the rule-breakers, the Hell's Angels of Ikea. You see, Ikea has one rule: YOU MUST FOLLOW THE ARROWS. If you don't, you could die by middle-class stampede. The arrows bring you through the past, present and future of your life. It's the river of self-construction that will eventually lead you to the Promised Land of the pick-up point. Follow the yellow arrows and they will show you what your one-bed studio apartment would look like. Move on, and there are two-seater couches and queen-sized beds, because now you're in a couple. Oh, look, the arrows have led us to a perfectly well-kept nursery and children's bedroom. Oh my God, I think, how did they know I needed a desk to work from home on? Seriously, I will be disappointed if, at some stage, I don't get to the checkouts to find they have self-assembly coffins.

This time, though, I got sucked into Ikea and started writing down the numbers on the yellow slips, just in case. I looked at a vinyl storage cupboard that I thought would look cool. Wrote it down. I looked at an Eames chair knock-off. Wrote it down. It was therapeutic. Retail therapy, without the purchase. Like people who fill the basket when they shop online and then empty it. I do it all the time on Apple's website. I buy the most expensive computer with all the bells and whistles. Once, I configured a desktop computer worth over €10,000, the type of computer that could edit *Lord of the Rings*. However, I forgot to empty my basket. Weeks later I had to buy a €25 cable and checked out, forgetting that I still had the €10,000 desktop computer in the basket. Several extremely panicky phone calls later, I had cancelled the purchase.

The one thing my wife constantly slags me about is my single-man mentality, even though we now have three kids. As we reach the one-bedroom apartment part of the shop she always tells me, 'Go in there, Bernard, you could find a few ideas for your fantasy.' My 'fantasy' being my own one-bed apartment in town. I always laugh it off, but it's true. Ikea show flats are perfect: on one condition – you never buy anything and don't move anything about. I could live in one, even with thousands of people walking through it between the hours of 9 a.m. to 6 p.m. All I would need is one drawer for my underwear and socks. (I have very particular tastes in underwear and socks. They are not very sexy, but they are very warm and practical.) My telly would face the bed and there would be just enough room for my laptop and guitar. Perfect.

Lorna constantly says to friends, 'I know Bernard would never cheat on me; he's too lazy and would much prefer his own company, playing his guitar and watching football.' This is one hundred per cent true. In my opinion, if you're contemplating an affair, you should consider the following three ideas as alternative options.

Number One: Going to the cinema. ON YOUR OWN. It is one of the joys of life that I didn't appreciate when I was childless. I would wander into the cinema during the day, when it was empty. I'd peruse all the films at my leisure and randomly judge people who spent over ten euros on pick and mix. Truly one of my greatest moments on planet Earth was when I saw *There Will be Blood*, *The Assassination of Jesse James by the Coward Robert Ford* and *No Country for Old Men*, all in one week. There were only a handful of people in each cinema. No one munching popcorn or talking, just three of the best films ever made being totally enjoyed and not ruined by people masticating.

The last time I went to the cinema was, at the time of writing, three months ago. We brought Tadhg and Olivia to see *Thomas and the Magic Railroad*. The fact that Thomas the Tank Engine travelled around the world and didn't need tracks didn't bemuse my children – however, having to bring Olivia to the toilet four times and Tadhg to the shop twice, just so he could look at a picture of a dinosaur stuck on a Slurpee machine, made me long to go on my own.

Number Two: Going to a restaurant. ON YOUR OWN. When I was single, I used to think it was embarrassing to sit down for a meal on your own. I used to think that the waiters and waitresses would be secretly judging me, whispering into each other's ears at the till: 'He must have no friends,' and 'I'll bet he'll try and chat me up because he's so lonely and pitiful.' Now, I can only dream of a paranoid luncheon date with myself. For starters (yes, pun intended), now that I'm dining with the kids, I have to clear the table of all knives, forks, glass and centrepieces. It's almost as if a bar-room brawl is about to start and you're clearing the table of all weapons first. My kids are obsessed with water in restaurants, and ice. You always know if the person serving has small children by how quickly they take the large jug of water off the table. Now, I also have to chop up and cool down all my kids' food before it's eaten and keep saying loudly, to the clear annoyance of other patrons, 'GET DOWN, GET DOWN, GET DOWN FROM THERE, NOW.' 'There' could be anywhere. They will decide to stand on anything as long as it's not their own seat.

I used to despise people with kids in restaurants: now, I am one of those parents who gladly puts Netflix on my phone for them as soon as a row kicks off about who's getting to sit beside Mammy. I dream of the days when I didn't have to go to the toilet four times with a five-year-old or eat my dinner like a velociraptor, just so my wife can hand me a baby to wind. I do love our family outings, but it would be nice just to eat my dinner, safe in the knowledge that someone isn't going to pour a beaker of diluted orange into it.

Number Three: Sitting in an empty room, ON YOUR OWN, doing nothing. I have to stress that THIS IS NOT

MEDITATION OR MINDFULNESS. It's just sitting, on your own, in a room, doing nothing. When I used to stay in nice hotels during a comedy tour, I would always wonder to myself what the big rooms with just chairs and books in them were for. Why would you pay money to sit in a room with nothing but big old furniture? Now I know why. Big old furniture isn't going to ask you to get it something the second you sit down. Big old furniture isn't going to ask you to wipe it. Walk past any day lounge in a hotel and it's an infirmary of worn-out individuals shell-shocked from a barrage of pick-ups and misfired yoghurt tubes.

All of these things I would fall in love with, but not another woman.

I was standing in my one-bed flat in Ikea and heard the call: 'Bernard, come on.' Now Olivia says it too. I picked Tadhg up and we headed off to the pick-up points. I found the two separate parts of Lorna's desk (of course, it would be in two separate parts). We headed to the checkout. It was full of families exactly like us, just desperate to get home and put together the plywood panels that would hopefully change their lives.

When we got outside, I could see the hope in people's eyes, but I just wanted to scream at them, 'You have to put this stuff together yourself.' I'm pretty sure that, if I weren't in a stable relationship, I'd be outside Ikea every day like a religious freak, telling people that the shop is evil. 'Don't go in there – you'll only come out with an Allen key that will take days off your life.'

When we got to the car, I opened the boot and had the realisation that our flatpack mightn't fit into it. As is traditional with all Ikea furniture, it was exactly 0.5 mm too big to get into the boot. However, there is an Irish solution to this Swedish problem. I forced it in with my thickness and bad temper. As it eventually hit the boot floor, with four disgruntled dog-ears on each corner and three disgruntled passengers waiting for their failure of a father to get in the car, I thought, 'Ireland one – Sweden nil.' I might possibly have celebrated too soon, however, as what goes into one's boot has to come out, so, after exactly three hours and forty minutes (calculated by my wife) her flatpack desk, in two badly bruised brown cardboard boxes, was strung across our bed like a naked Picasso.

Lorna and I had previous with flatpack construction. Forget your pre-marriage courses: make a couple who are getting married put a piece of Ikea furniture together. The last time we tried this, I actually thought she was going to stab me with the free flat-head screwdriver that came with the set of drawers.

It had started off light-heartedly, then became slightly serious. 'You're supposed to put it into 6F and then go underneath' progressed to 'Bernard, just leave it, you're going to break it.' I did. If it was a romantic comedy, we would have ended up in bed together laughing it off. However, in a small flat with a screaming newborn, you just end up screaming at each other, 'Well, you do it then, if you're so f##king smart.'

So this time round, I was determined to make the right decision from the start. I self-elected myself to assemble the desk. Lorna lovingly said, 'No, you're absolutely useless at these things,' which only showed me how much she wanted to motivate me into doing it. After a brief fight over her begging me to 'follow the f##king instructions, Bernard', I got going. I opened the two boxes and started to lay out all the pieces on the bed. Then I got the instructions. The little drawing of the person on the pages looked so reassuring. The large bold type repeating, 'Do not use a drill or hammer' injected me with a powerful strain of liquid I like to call 'nonfidence'. Nonfidence is a word I've coined to describe the feeling of confidence that comes with having no ability whatsoever. In this instance, I had massive confidence in my ability to assemble the Ikea desk, in spite of having absolutely no DIY skills.

Another example of my nonfidence would be talking to builders or car mechanics. I have no knowledge of how to build a wall, or fix an engine, but I will talk about it in absolute confidence. Nonfidence is extremely helpful if, for example, you feel like you're being conned on your car service: 'What? Two hundred euros to change the oil? I could do it myself for twenty.' However, it makes life extremely difficult when you do try and do it yourself and end up flooding the engine and doing fifteen thousand euros' worth of damage.

It only took about a quarter of an hour before I threw away the instructions for assembling the Ikea desk. The whole business of 'place 6F into slot A' wasn't working for me, so I got rid of them. Fast forward ten minutes and I had got the power tools out; another five and I had a lump hammer.

What is sold to you as self-assembly is actually self-assessment. Those finely cut pieces of Swedish mulch aren't fitting together because they are judging you. Every time a reverse screw won't catch to the incline of the weight of the left-facing leg, Sweden is roaring at you: 'You are not a man; you are just a stupid red-haired afterthought of European humanity.' The Allen key had now burned my hand from the number of turns I had done on one particular screw because I had worn out the thread. It was time to get serious. Enter the nail gun. At this stage, my wife was actually crying. 'Why couldn't you just follow the instructions?' Why? I'll tell you why – because no amount of instructions can defeat me.

Why did they have it in two parts? They would just not join together. No amount of instructions could explain how the two halves became one. I banished her from the room. Now, more than ever, I was determined to create. Little did she, or I, know that what was about to happen next would be chilling.

Three hours in and night settled upon me. There was an eeriness about the place. Sweat trickled down my back, while a crow hawked angrily in the distance. A harsh clap of powerful thunder shuddered in the trees, even though there were no trees within a three-mile radius. A burst of lightning lit up the room. I stood away from my creation and laughed hysterically. Before me, a monster. I thought to myself, 'When falsehood can look so like the truth, who can assure themselves of certain happiness?'

Then the desk spoke: 'Kill me, please.'

Just then, my wife walked in. 'No,' I screamed, 'You can't see him; he is not of this earth.'

She looked at me and cried, 'You have a created a monster, a monster that we cannot use or bring back to Ikea,' and with that, my creation was borne away by the waves and lost in darkness and distance.

The next day my wife went to Ikea and bought the desk again. It only came in one box. She assembled it in under half an hour with just an Allen key. Apparently, I had bought a desk and a vinyl storage cupboard and tried to fuse them together. 'Apparently', in this case, being exactly what I did. What compounded my insecurities was that she was able to place her books and heavy objects like staplers on it almost immediately, while feeding Tadhg a bottle and doing an online Tesco shop.

Did I learn a valuable lesson about patience and allowing my wife to take over all DIY projects in our home? No, I did not. I continued trying to make my furniture monster into a drinks cabinet, until one day I came home from work and found that Lorna had brought it to the dump. We still have that desk. And no matter how hard I try to break it with my lump hammer, whatever way she put it together, it won't break. She insists that she 'just followed the instructions', but I know there's some wife voodoo at play. Instructions, indeed – she's just trying to put me off the scent.

Afterword

I t's time for an apology. I spend a lot of time apologising to Lorna, but there are a few apologies my wife particularly deserves, including some for what I am about to do.

It sounds odd to apologise for things that haven't happened yet. Not for me. As you've probably guessed by now, I'm a repeat reoffender and I know what I'll have to apologise for in the future so I might as well get to it now:

In my forties, I will be sorry for:

* Buying a family car that has only two seats in the back, even though we have three children. I will try to argue that the kids will be old enough to take the bus.
* Forgetting to pick up one of the kids from the pool or a lesson. I get confused easily and always find two or more pick-ups hard.
* Dressing too young for my age. I have a fear of growing old. This is why I will also spend money on a hair transplant.

In my fifties, I will be sorry for:

* Not wanting to go out: I'm not able for the loud music any more. You're only able until your mid-forties, then it's curtains.

* Telling one of the kids to move out of the house.
* Constantly giving out about my dodgy hair transplant.

In my sixties, I will be sorry for:

* Making Lorna drive everywhere. Give me a break: I'm in my sixties.
* Not sharing Lorna's enthusiasm for caravanning. You can stay in one; I'll be booking into a hotel.
* Hopefully letting Lorna do all the work with our grandkids and not helping.

In my seventies:

* I plan to have a midlife crisis, so I'll be heading out on the town with the grandkids. Don't wait up, Lorna, and you can come if you like.

In my eighties:

* I hope we're still fighting.